Dec. 1981

Dear John,

This should give you some idea of what a small computer can and cannot do.

Merry Christmas!
Connie

The Small Computer in Small Business

The Small Computer

A Guide to Selection and Use

in Small **Business**

Brian R. Smith

MANAGEMENT CONSULTANT AND
DIRECTOR OF EDUCATION,
COUNTRY BUSINESS SERVICES

THE STEPHEN GREENE PRESS
BRATTLEBORO, VERMONT

The Small Computer in Small Business by BRIAN R. SMITH

Text copyright © 1981 by BRIAN R. SMITH.
Illustrations copyright © 1981 by THE STEPHEN GREENE PRESS.

This book has been produced in the United States of America.
It is designed by IRVING PERKINS ASSOCIATES, and published by THE STEPHEN GREENE PRESS, Fessenden Road, Brattleboro, Vermont 05301.

PUBLISHED JANUARY 1981
Second printing February 1981

Library of Congress Cataloging in Publication Data
SMITH, BRIAN R.   1939–
 The small computer in small business.

 Bibliography: p.
 Includes index.
 1. Business–Data processing.   2. Small business–
Data processing.   3. Minicomputer.   I. Title.
HF5548.2.S56   658'.022'02854   80–20734
ISBN 0–8289–0407–3

To Adam, my son

Contents

Acknowledgments

I want to take the opportunity to thank some of the people who helped to make this book possible. Many individuals in computer-related firms who sent materials to me or chatted with me on the phone, or both, appear in the text. If the mention of their company's name brings them added business I will feel gratified that I have reciprocated the favors they have done for me.

Three people served as catalysts for this book: James Howard, president of Country Business Services in Brattleboro, Vermont; Allan Kendall, owner of Allan Kendall's Office Specialties in Keene, New Hampshire; and Bob Vitelli, who was a student of mine at Franklin Pierce College in Rindge, New Hampshire. My thanks to all of them and especially to Jim Howard and his staff for much continuing support throughout the entire effort.

As the book took shape, more individuals helped with their suggestions and input. Jim Lockley, president of National Software Exchange in East St. Louis, made a number of suggestions on the book as a whole, and Lon Poole of Osborne/McGraw-Hill furnished me with an entire software book that his firm produces. Jeff Dando, the marketing manager of Computer Management Dynamics of Nashua, New Hampshire, had numerous helpful suggestions. Special thanks go to Charlie Collette, one of the country's leading experts in small computer technology, for his technical review of the completed text.

Finally, I would like to thank the fine folks at The Stephen Greene Press, especially Castle Freeman who saw me through the entire process.

B.R.S.

xi

Introduction: The Small Computer
in Small Business

The age of the electronic data processing machine, *aka* the computer, has arrived in full array. Although there are still many things to accomplish in the field of computer technology, it is safe to say that the small computer—those systems costing around $25,000 or less—is now ready to become an integral part of businesses grossing $100,000 or more in annual sales. Many entrepreneurs and business owners have made the transition to relying on a computer already, some with magnificent success and others with utter failure.

Most of the failures can be traced to business owners making the decision to take on a computer based on inadequate or faulty information. These owners did not spend enough time in research before installing their computers, and, as a result, they made unrealistic assumptions about what the machines could do for them, and when.

In one respect, a computer is just another machine that has the potential to help you conduct your business more efficiently and profitably. Repeat: *has the potential to help* . . . Although technology moves rapidly in the computer field, it has not yet reached the state where a computer can be brought into a business, turned on, and immediately and without human intervention, begin working at its fullest capacity. A computer is a complex electronic and mechanical device that requires a commitment of time and effort on the part of those who would benefit from what it can do, as much as it requires a commitment of money.

Computers have changed radically from the scientific curiosities of the late

1940's that used vacuum tubes and weighed several tons, to powerful machines that use circuitry too small to be seen with the naked eye and weigh only several pounds. Small business today seems to be about where large business was 15 or 20 years ago—the majority of small-business owners have heard about computers and think that they might be able to use one, but most are a little reluctant to jump right in and get going because of a basic fear that stems from lack of knowledge about computers. This book is intended to dispel those fears by providing that knowledge.

Ever since I saw my first computer in 1959 as an engineering undergraduate, I have been fascinated by what these electronic marvels can do. But I am not a computer "expert." I can't program them, and I can't fix them. My major field of expertise is small business. In looking over the books available to small-businessowners about the small computer, however, I found most of them to be so loaded with technical jargon as to be of little practical use to computer laymen. These books were written by computer people, not business people. A couple of the publications were nearly unintelligible. I therefore wrote *The Small Computer in Small Business* to be a primer for business operators or entrepreneurs who want to gain a basic knowledge of computers in order to be able to deal with computer vendors. I assume that the reader knows very little about data processing, so I have tried to keep the gobbledygook to an absolute minimum.

Some books speak of **minicomputers** and **microcomputers,** but I have chosen to use the term "small computer" and leave it at that. The price range of the small computers discussed in this book will be from $2,500 to $25,000, including the **programs** that make the machine function.

A weak point of some other books in this area is that many of them make reference to specific suppliers of **hardware** (machines) and **software** (programs). Any such list of firms would be obsolete the day it is published because of the rapid changes in the field. Although I do mention a few names here and there, these names have been carefully selected on the basis of their longevity in the computer field.

I have tried as best I could to let the book flow in a logical fashion and to let each chapter build on information that was presented in earlier sections. Also, I have not spent much time in the way of teaching you about programming—a mistake that I feel other authors have made. There are oodles of programming books around that do a much better job than I could ever do.

The glossary in Appendix D should help you with computer terms used in this book and other terms that you may hear in the trade. In the text, terms that are set in **boldface** type are explained in the glossary.

This book is intended to be easy to read and to understand. I also hope that you gain something from the book in the way of knowledge, and that it helps you to make a choice in what you want to do, even if your decision is not to purchase a computer at this point.

B.R.S.

The Small Computer in Small Business

Chapter **1** What Is a Computer?

Computers of one kind or another have been around for centuries. Many civilizations invented devices to assist them with mathematical calculations (the *abacus, soroban, suan-pan, choty*). The electronic computer, however, the subject of this book, has been in existence for only about thirty-five years, and in practical business use for a little over twenty years. During this period, the electronic computer has become a household item, and is very rapidly making its appearance in small business.

Most of us know by now—or we should know—what a computer is. Many others, however, even computer "experts," don't know what a computer is *not*. There are many misconceptions about this marvelous machine, but that's all it is—a machine. It cannot "think," by any adequate definition of thought. It cannot, in and of itself, generate thought. A computer must be told, through a series of instructions called a **program**, what to do. Once told what to do, it blindly follows instructions until it reaches the end of the program.

There is a sign that many computer specialists have hanging over their desks. It reads, "Computers Cannot Think—Yet."

Smith's Laws

Since computers cannot think in the same way that humans do, we are led to Smith's First Law of Computers:

A computer is not a species.

Computers should not be referred to as "electronic brains," as they were in the 1950's. It is true that man and the computer are working closely together—their relationship could even be called symbiotic—but for our purposes, we will not conceive of computers as living, thinking beings. They cannot reproduce their own kind.

Another common misconception about computers is closely aligned with the fallacy that computers can act on their own. We have all heard someone state that "the computer" sent him such-and-such a bill or report. Although the statement is probably technically correct (in that the bill was produced by a computer and prepared on a computer's printer), it gives the impression that a computer is capable of much more than it really can do. Smith's Second Law of Computers states:

A computer is nothing more than a very fast, very "dumb," adding machine.

This statement, though it oversimplifies the internal workings of the machine, is a good concept to keep in mind. Some people will say that a computer is nothing more than a logical decision-making device—it can decide if one number is larger than another—but the process still boils down to basic addition (subtraction is negative addition, multiplication is repetitive addition, and division is repetitive subtraction).

Smith's Third Law of Computers states:

A computer *never* makes a mistake.

Some people may take exception to that statement, but think of it as a working premise rather than an indisputable law. The times the computer itself actually makes an internal error are so few that the law will hold for all practical purposes. When mistakes are made, they are normally the fault of the person who wrote the program for the machine, not of the machine itself.

Calculator or Computer?

Is a typical $10 calculator a computer in the true sense? After all, it does compute. It can usually store a few numbers, too. But the answer is No, a calculator is not a computer. For one thing, the calculator cannot repeat a series of instructions. In the second place, it cannot make a **logical decision** ("logical" in this context does not mean that the decision makes sense, it means that the decision is governed by the laws of mathematical **logic**, of which more will be said later).*

For example, suppose that the town in which you live has a regulation which states that people over 65 get a red identification card that enables them to ride the public transportation system free. Assume that today is your 64th birthday and you want to see if you can ride the bus free. On your 64th birthday, you have been alive for 23,376 days.† If today were your 65th birthday, you would have lived *another* 365 days, for a total of 23,741 days. You call up City Hall, and after getting about 14 wrong departments you finally land the person who gives out the senior citizen transit cards. He asks you how old you are. You respond, "Today is my 64th birthday."

Now suppose the transit-card clerk has both a calculator and a computer. His instructions on receiving an application like yours are to first calculate your eligibility with the calculator and then to check the result on the computer. If the final answer is negative, you cannot get a red card. If the answer is zero, they can take your name and address but cannot give out the card until the next day. If the result is positive, they can process the information and issue the card.

Both the calculator and the computer have the number 23,741 stored in memory.

The Calculator

To compute the answer, the clerk performs the following operations:

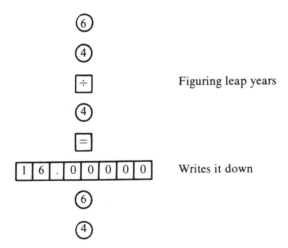

6
4
÷   Figuring leap years
4
=
1 6 . 0 0 0 0 0   Writes it down
6
4

---

* Some experts make the further distinction that a computer can automatically call in data from some device like a magnetic tape or **disk,** operate on that data, and then create its own output. This is clearly beyond the capacity of our $10 calculator.
† This figure includes 16 leap years.

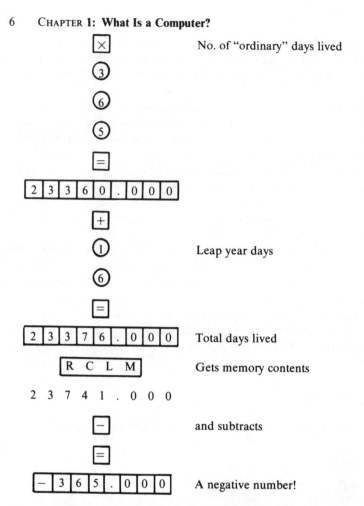

No. of "ordinary" days lived

Leap year days

Total days lived

Gets memory contents

and subtracts

A negative number!

The appearance of a negative number means that no card can be issued.

The Computer

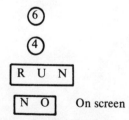

On screen

Sorry, no card today!

What did the computer do? It did all the steps that the calculator did but with two significant differences:

1. It did all the operations automatically without any intervention.
2. When the computer saw the negative number, -365, it was able to show the answer "NO." It would have been able to do other things if the answer was "0" or a positive number, like actually issuing the card itself.

Computers Defined

A computer has been defined by the **American National Standards Institute (ANSI)** as a "device capable of performing systematic sequences of operation upon data, including numerous arithmetic and logic procedures, without intervention by a human operator during the run."

So computers can do things automatically, like issue free-ride cards to senior citizens, do your payroll, guide ships to the stars, or tell you how many birds you can catch with all the salt in the ocean.

Useful? You bet!

Hard to understand? No!

Analog and Digital Computers

Computers are classified in two categories—digital and analog. The digital computer is the breed that most of us are familiar with; it calculates quantities in much the same way that we do and then expresses the answers in the desired, readable way we specify.

Our hand-held calculators, although not computers (some come very close), are the best examples of the computational method of digital computers. When we strike the following keys

the answer, "7," appears on the small lighted screen.

Analog computers, on the other hand, represent physical quantities such as time, weight, and volume with mechanical or electrical analogs. The speedometer of a car is a perfect example. The rotational speed of one of the shafts in the transmission is translated to other rotations until the final result is "read" as we drive.

This book will not be concerned with any analog computers except the various electrical analogs within the digital machine that represent actual numbers as both we and the computer understand them (more on this later when we discuss the theory of operation of a typical digital computer).

Small Computers

The electronic computer has changed radically in the thirty-five or so years of its existence. Basically, the device has gotten smaller, faster, cheaper, and more capable than its early predecessors (see Table 1.1). It has changed from a highly technical device that could be used only by sophisticated engineers, mathematicians, and scientists, to a machine that is now found in many homes and businesses (see Figure 1.1). Soon, people will be carrying computers around in attaché cases. Several models already have this capability.

Figure 1.1 *A small computer with a full complement of input/output equipment (from left to right): printer, workstation (CRT and keyboard), floppy disk drive (dual), hard disk drive. Courtesy of Wang Laboratories, Inc., Tewksbury, Mass.*

TABLE 1.1

Development of Computer and Auto over 30 Years
(NOTE: Money values in the 1950 column are for dollars at their 1950 valuation.)

Typical Car	*1950*	*1980*
Weight	3000 lbs	3000 lbs
Speed (cruising)	60 mph	60 mph
Cost	$2,500	$9,000
Typical Computer		
Weight	30,000 lbs	30 lbs
Speed (adding 2 numbers)	0.001 second	0.00000000001 sec
Cost	$3,000,000	$3,000

There are probably two million small computers in use around the world, with more on the way. The small computer market, consisting of **hardware** (the physical units) and **software** (written instructions for computer operations, contained within programs), is one of the most rapidly growing in the world. Of the nine million small businesses in the United States, fully 50 percent could make good use of their own small computer today.

Chapter 2 How Computers Work

This chapter is divided into three sections, on computer theory, components, and data processing. In no section will we go into a great amount of technical detail. The purpose of this book is to acquaint entrepreneurs and existing small-business owners with aspects of computer technology that are relevant to business, more than it is to inform them on the workings of computers themselves. For any reader who needs more technical information, there are many books on the market that go into detail on computer theory and operation (some are listed in the bibliography in Appendix C).

Theory

Basically, computers manipulate data that have been encoded as numbers. They perform, electrically and at high speed, simple operations on numerical data, employing a special **binary** system of numbering that reflects the off-or-on condition of the computer's circuitry.

Numbering Systems and the Computer

Numbering systems are "notations"—ways of counting, or of writing down quantities. Different numbering systems are chosen arbitrarily, or because of their convenience for a specific purpose. Most of us operate in the "base 10" system. This means that, in our written notations, every time we reach ten or any higher number that is evenly divisible by ten (100, 1,000) we shift notation one place to the left.

$$1, \ 2, \ 3, \ 4, \ 5, \ 6, \ 7, \ 8, \ 9, \ \textit{10}$$

Look at the last number. It has two digits—a one and a zero. We could have written the same number in other ways. We could have written it

$$1 \ 1 \ 1 \ 1 \ 1 \ 1 \ 1 \ 1 \ 1 \ 1$$

or we could have written it

$$11111 \qquad 11111$$

or

$$9 + 1$$

We use the base 10 numbering system because we have ten fingers. Some people work in the base 8, which, as Tom Lehrer says, is just like the base 10 if you're missing two fingers. Let's count to 10 in base 8:

$$1, \ 2, \ 3, \ 4, \ 5, \ 6, \ 7, \ \textit{10}, \ 11, \ 12,$$

In base 8 there is no number 8 or 9. You shift one place to the left each time you hit the base—8—or any even multiple of the base.

Computers like the binary system, or base 2. Base 2 has only two digits, 0 and 1. Let's count to ten in base 2:

$$1, \ 10, \ 11, \ 100, \ 101, \ 110, \ 111, \ 1000, \ 1001, \ 1010$$

We wouldn't want to work every day in the binary system. It's too cumbersome. Consider a small city with population 19,947. In binary notation the figure would be written, 100110111101011.

Notice, however, that a two-digit number system is tailor-made for the way an electronic device must count and calculate; for the two-digit system corresponds with the nature of the device's electronic circuitry, in which a voltage is either present or not, a circuit either "on" or "off." The computer would carry the population of our little city as

on-off-off-on-on-off-on-on-on-on-off-on-off-on-on

(where 1 means "on," which means "voltage is present"; and 0 means "off," which means "no voltage is present").

How Computers Compute

We said earlier in the book that a computer is really a very fast adding machine. A computer can perform binary addition because of the laws of physics, the concepts of zero (no voltage) and one (a voltage present), and circuitry that has been designed to route electrical signals in a certain way (Figure 2.1). Consider an electrical switch in its open state:

If there is a signal at point A, there will be no signal at point B because the electrical connection is open or broken. If the switch were closed then the signal would pass freely from A to B:

Now assume that the switches are arranged like this:

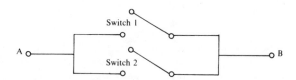

Still no signal can pass from A to B. If either switch 1 or switch 2 is closed (or both), then a signal can be passed successfully from A to B. This arrangement is known as an **or** device (or gate) and is drawn as follows:

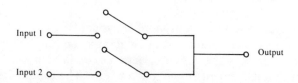

The rule for the operation of an *or* gate is:

> If either or both of the two inputs has a signal or voltage present (a 1), then there is a signal or voltage present at the output.

Therefore, there are four distinct and separate possibilities with an *or* gate:

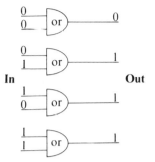

Now, we need to define a function called **and** which says that if both inputs are "1," then the result is "1," otherwise it is "0." The *and* device is:

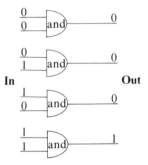

A *nor* (not *or*) and *nand* (not *and*) simply reverse the stated rules for *or* and *and*, respectively, and a *not* device changes a 1 to a 0 and vice versa.

Figure 2.1 *Typical computer circuitry representing the processing segment of a small computer. Courtesy of Digital Equipment Corporation.*

The Half-Adder. The basic computational device within a computer is a piece of circuitry known as a **half-adder**. The half-adder follows the basic rules for adding in the binary system:

$$1 + 0 = 01 \quad \text{and} \quad 1 + 1 = 10$$

where 1 is the presence of an electrical signal and 0 is the absence of one.

Figures 2.2 and 2.3 show a half-adder performing the basic rules. All other mathematical operations, decisions, and the carrying of letters and symbols are done in much the same way. As we said before, there are books on the market that get into the theory of operation in more detail, if you want to go more deeply into the matter.

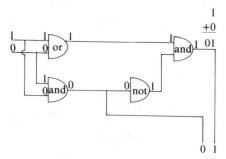

Figure 2.2 *A half-adder performing 1 + 0 = 01.*

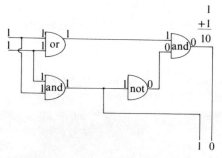

Figure 2.3 *A half-adder performing 1 + 1 = 10.*

Components

Internal Workings

Half-adders are the basic computational hardware pieces. An early computer, Howard Aiken's MARK I (circa 1944), required about seven relays, each weighing a pound or so, to perform basic binary addition. We can now squeeze

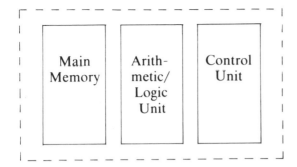

Figure 2.4 *Central processing unit (CPU).*

millions of these devices into a square inch. This computational or **arithmetic/ logic unit** of the entire computer is only *one* part of *one* major unit. It is a part of the **central processing unit** or **CPU** shown diagrammatically in Figure 2.4.

The arithmetic unit usually has other chores besides calculations. It:

- Locates needed things, such as numbers or instructions, within other parts of the CPU.
- Puts items into the memory that should be there—your name, address and how much you owe on a bill so it can send you nasty, impersonal letters.
- Decodes instructions from the way they were written to the way it understands things.
- Sequences itself as it executes a program.
- Examines things that you tell it to do and lets you know when you told it to do something it can't.
- Keeps time.

In Figure 2.4 there are two other units, the **main memory** and the **control unit.** We will talk about the memory first.

If you listen to computer freaks, you will hear such semantic atrocities as **byte,** "13K," "64K." These are not new Internal Revenue Service regulations; they refer to the size of a computer's main memory in thousands of bytes. What's a byte? It's an eight-"letter" word (usually) in which the letters are binary numbers, or **bits** (*bit* = "*bi*nary digi*t*"). (Half of a byte, or four bits, is known as a **nibble,** also spelled **nybble.**)

Remember the 0's and 1's from the section on binary notation? Suppose I want to store your age somewhere permanently in the main memory of the computer. If you are 36 years old, your age will be written using eight bits:

0	0	1	0	0	1	0	0
off	off	on	off	off	on	off	off

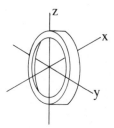

Figure 2.5 *One magnetic core (one bit).*

That is one byte. If the machine is a "64K machine," it has the capability of storing 65,536 (2 to the 16th power) bytes, or 512,000 bits. If you are looking over various machines, the size of the main memory should be of some concern to you, but should not be overpowering. A 4K machine is usually of insufficient size for most small businesses. With today's prices, a 64K machine should be a minimum memory size, but be certain that the salesperson or technical representative fully explains the machine's operating features. Some machines use temporary storage like a **disk** and then call that data back when it is required.

The cost of memory has gone from huge to peanuts in 20 years. Back in the 1950's, main memory could be constructed only by nimble-fingered people stringing small doughnut-like wheels of iron onto even smaller wires as shown in Figure 2.5.

Lots of people went whacko doing that. Today it's a different story (see Figure 2.6), but the principle of operation is the same: if a memory **location** has been electrically energized it represents a 1, otherwise a zero.

To understand the control unit, we need to look at Figure 2.7.

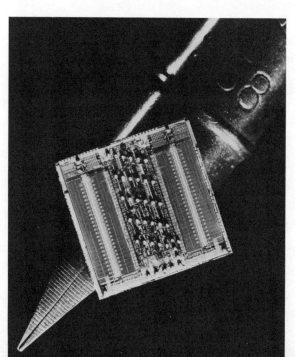

Figure 2.6 *This is a memory "chip" shown on the tip of a fountain pen. This one-quarter inch square element can store up to 64,000 bits of information—equivalent to about 1,000 eight-letter words. Courtesy of IBM Corporation.*

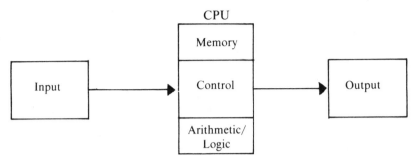

Figure 2.7 *A computer.*

When any signal (**input**) comes into the machine (like you tapping on the keyboard), the control unit has to know what to do with it. When it's time to display a result (the **output**), it has to know when to do that, also. The control unit is the traffic cop of the computer—taking data, sending it to the main memory for a while, calling it out of memory to be used in a calculation, putting that result back into memory, calling out the final data to be printed for you.

All this data transfer takes place on an electrical device called a **bus.** Some machines have several buses (memory, input/output, selector, multiplexor, data) and some, like several of Digital Equipment Corporation's computers, use just one.

Input

The input device is just what the name implies. It is a piece of hardware that allows you to enter program instructions and data into the machine. The early IBM computers used an 80-column punched card like the thing your phone bill comes on to enter the computer. Later machines went to magnetic tape—big 2500-foot reels of half-inch stuff. Then disks were born. These are flat platters covered with brown iron oxide (advanced rust) that spin around and carry a world of data on them.

For your present state of knowledge, there are really only four important input media that you ought to be concerned with.

Keyboard Workstation. Everyone has used a typewriter. That is basically what you are doing with the keyboard but with a few new wrinkles. Each key on the **keyboard** may have as many as three different functions: a standard alphabetical **character**, a special character, and a command. Be sure to examine the keyboard of any machine that you are going to buy or rent to be sure it's relatively free from confusion. Remember, you may eventually be teaching this whole thing to Harry or Suzy. The keyboard is usually part of a screen that looks like a television set. This is a **cathode ray tube (CRT).** Its job is to show

Figure 2.8 *A group of workstations each consisting of a keyboard and CRT. Courtesy of Wang Laboratories, Inc., Tewksbury, Mass.*

Figure 2.9 *A workstation (CRT and keyboard) with two floppy disk drives to the right of the viewing screen. Courtesy of Pertec Computer Corporation.*

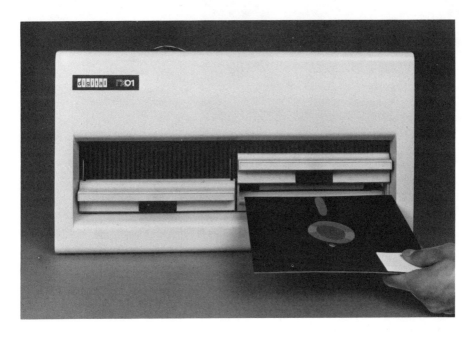

Figure 2.10 *An 8" floppy disk being inserted into a disk drive unit. Notice that just above the center hole on the disk itself there is a slot where data is either read or written. Courtesy of Digital Equipment Corporation.*

you what you have typed, and it may ask you things or it may tell you that you've done something bad.

Flexible Disk. This is also known as a **floppy disk.** It looks something like a 45-rpm record, and is actually meant to work while it is inside its jacket. To "write on the disk" does not mean that you take the disk out of its cardboard cover and make marks on it with a pencil, it means that the computer implants information on the disk. Floppies can hold anywhere from 200,000 to 3 million bytes (3 megabytes) depending on the disk's density.

Figure 2.11 shows the general construction of a disk.

Figure 2.11 *A disk (viewed from above).*

Tracks

Sector

Figure 2.12 *A removable hard disk (round plate-like object) and its drive unit. Courtesy of Wang Laboratories, Inc., Tewksbury, Mass.*

Disks usually have eight sectors (pie-pieces) and there may be a few hundred tracks which are one revolution around the disk. (Great way to win money at a cocktail party: Ask someone how many grooves there are on a 33⅓-rpm record that plays for twenty minutes. Answer: One!) The disk in its jacket usually measures 8 × 8 inches (although there are 5-inch and 3-inch types), and is usually driven about 90 rpm. Blank disks cost around $5 each. Floppy disk drives cost from $500 to $2500.

The machine you look at should have at least two floppy disk drives, and preferably four.

Hard Disks. The rigid or **hard disk** has been around much longer than the floppy disk, but until recently was reserved for use with large computers. Now hard disks are available for most of the smaller computers. They are quite a bit more expensive than floppy disk drives (costing from $3500 to $10,000) but they hold much more information (from 10 to 100 megabytes) and can access data more quickly. Before you buy a computer, you should analyze carefully the amount of data that you will be handling, because you may need a hard disk in addition to your floppies.

Another disk input system is the "Winchester disk," a device in which the disk itself is a part of the entire drive. The disk is not removable; it is fixed in place along with the device which reads data (the read head) and the electronics. It requires no preventive maintenance.

Hard disks are one of the latest pieces of input/output equipment to be developed for the small computer that give it the power and capability of its larger and more expensive cousins. It is very important that you determine *in the beginning* whether you will need a hard disk. It may be impossible for you to add it later.

Tape. Tape cartridges and **cassettes** are fine for junior and his recorder/ player but not for small computers. The main problem is that the access to information is sequential in nature rather than random, as is true for the disks. If you need to know how much money you owe ABC Distributors, finding out may take up to two minutes on some tapes, since the entire **file** will have to be searched, one **record** at a time, until the right one is found. The usual speed to find the same data on a disk is in fractions of a second. Still and all, tape is a cheaper way to go, but few small computers today use tapes in any form. The ones that do use tape are either the very inexpensive machines that are unsuited to most small businesses or ones that use the tape for "backing up" a disk— copying the contents of a disk.

In addition to these four common types of input devices, you should be aware of **audio response/recognition** and **optical character recognition (OCR)**.

Audio Response/Recognition. Some lusty entrepreneurs play around with such esoteric things as audio response/recognition units. These are fun toys but not very practical for small business applications yet. By 1984 they should be- come cost-effective, however. An audio unit can either recognize the human voice, or respond to signals with a recorded voice, or both. You may have had the experience of dialing a non-working telephone number. The operator will come on the line and ask, "What number are you dialing?" Suppose that you have dialed 336-5937, and that number has been changed to 336-7146. When you inform the operator of the number you originally dialed, each of the seven

Figure 2.13 *A tape cartridge (upper right), its drive unit (upper left), and the associated circuitry. Courtesy of Digital Equipment Corporation.*

digits is keyed into a computer. At that point, the operator hangs up and the computer takes over. You will hear the computer respond with: *"The number you have dialed, three-three-six-five-nine-three-seven, has been changed to three-three-six-seven-one-four-six."* Each of the words in the computer's message is stored on a drum or disk like a phonograph record, and the computer selects the proper words and "plays" them for you.

Optical Character Recognition. In addition to audio response/recognition, the computer industry has experimented with optical character recognition (OCR) for a long time, and has never gotten very far. OCR is the general capability of a computer to read the printed word. It may never be seen in small business, since the workstation (CRT and keyboard) in effect makes OCR unnecessary. The workstation makes the computer interactive or conversational in nature, allowing the computer to prompt you, the operator, with messages and questions, to which you respond with data or commands. The computer doesn't need to be able to read, for it can find out all it needs to know by asking you questions, so to speak.

Output

Any input device (except the keyboard itself) can usually be an output device. If you want, after you've done your monthly general ledger program, you can implant or **write** your financial statements on the disk. Then, when your banker asks for May's profit and loss statements, should you scale a floppy disk across the office at him? Not bloody likely. He wants something he can read, so you'll need a printer of some kind to provide him with a **hard copy.** Output onto the CRT for temporary visual inspection is called **soft copy.** An operator can display hundreds of characters on one screen in a fraction of a second without a single sound or motion. The problem is that if the data is to be retained it must be copied down by hand. Some people have tried taking a picture of it but the flash washes out the screen and they have wound up with dozens of color photographs of a green rectangle.

HINT: Get a printer.

Most small computers will come with a printer. There are two general types: keyboard and line. The first type resembles an electric typewriter. It is slow as molasses going uphill (10 to 30 characters per second) but cheap and reliable. Many people use a standard Teletype machine, which can be had for under $1000. These things are fine as long as you don't need special jobs done (like paychecks) or a lot of data printed.

Line printers, the second type, are faster—up to 300 lines per minute—and more expensive—up to five times the cost of a character printer. Some printers have a type chain or wheel, some blow ink on the paper, others use an electrostatic process. Most use what is known as a 5-by-7 dot matrix pattern to create

Figure 2.14 *Shown here are three printers. The two on the table are character printers which resemble typewriters and are capable of printing 30 characters per second. Note that the printer to the left has tractor feed—see the holes in the sides of the paper. The printer in the foreground can operate at speeds up to 180 characters per second. Courtesy of Digital Equipment Corporation.*

numbers, letters, and special characters. Figure 2.15 shows a representative sample of matrix patterns.

Figure 2.15 *Sample 5-by-7 dot matrix patterns.*

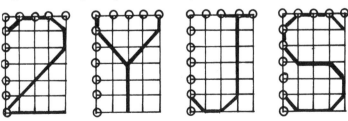

Figure 2.16 *A full-duplex modem capable of transmission speeds of 1200 bits per second using a standard telephone. Courtesy of Anderson Jacobson, Inc., San Jose, Calif.*

Other Devices. Unless there is a very good reason, stay away from the following:

- Punched cards (except ones sent to you by the utility companies).
- Paper tape (at last check, Singer-Friden was still trying to revive this market. Let's hope they don't make it).
- Plotters (expensive toys).
- Magnetic ink readers (leave them to the banks).
- Mark-sense readers (remember the second grade IQ test that you took with pencils so soft that you're still cleaning the graphite from under your fingernails?)
- Used stuff. (Forget fire sales on EDP equipment. Get new machinery. It's cheaper in the long run.)

Before we leave this section of Chapter 2, we should say a word about data transmission. This paragraph is only for those of you who have more than one business location and need to transmit data from one location to another. In the first place, be certain that you really need to send the information over telephone lines or (worse yet) a private circuit. If your other shoe store is only two miles across town, pick up the cash register data when you go there, or have someone drop it off. And don't be so cute that you put a terminal in your home to impress your friends. If you honestly do need to transmit data, you will need a **modulator/demodulator (modem)** on each end of the phone line as shown in Figures 2.16 and 2.17.

24

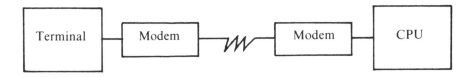

Figure 2.17 *Remote processing.*

A modem is simply a device which converts the computer's electronic signals to audible sounds (or vice versa) that can be transmitted over a normal voice-type telephone line. For instance, if you call the computer on the phone, it "answers" by beeping at you. You can then transmit your data. Computers with this capability are more expensive, however.

Some machines are capable of remote processing, which means that you can physically move the CRT some distance away from the CPU (see Figure 2.18). This often means stringing a line between the two devices and if your luck is like mine, either Mrs. Murphy will hang her wash on it or Fido will bite it.

Figure 2.18 *Workstations being used remotely from the main computer. Courtesy of Data General Corporation.*

Data Processing

Previously we covered what computers are (and aren't) and a little about how they work. Now we are going to spend some time on the manipulation of raw alphabetical and numerical (called **alphanumerical**) information by an electronic machine to produce new information that is of greater use to the business owner than it was in its original state. That's what electronic data processing or **EDP** is all about. We will tend to use "data" and "information" somewhat interchangeably when, in fact, there is a difference. *Data* are raw facts, whereas *information* is processed data. Suppose, for example, that you have one of the thermometers which automatically records the highest and the lowest temperature of the day. If you kept up this procedure for some period of time (a year, for instance) you would have a collection of data. If you compiled a report for your local newspaper which gave the *average* temperature for each month, that's information.

Figure 2.19 *A computer processing data. The woman in the picture is working with invoicing procedures. Courtesy of Digital Equipment Corporation.*

You are a data processor. If I were to come into your business and ask about Sam Henderson, you might respond with something like, "He's owed me $40.00 for over two months." You took Sam's name (input data), automatically decoded it so that your brain could use the data, searched your memory, encoded the information that you found and then told me something about Sam (output information). A computer could have done the same thing, as long as you told it that you wanted to find out if Sam Henderson owed any money or not.

Suppose you held a job as a payroll clerk. To start you off, we would equip you with a standard calculator and a typewriter. Then we would give you detailed instructions about your job:

1. You will periodically receive time cards for each employee stating how many hours they have worked in a week.
2. You will keep a permanent file of the hourly pay rate for all employees.
3. To calculate gross pay, multiply the employee's hourly rate by the number of hours worked, unless they have worked more than 40 hours in a week in which case they receive one and one-half their hourly rate for all time over 40 hours.
4. The withholding rate totals 25 percent of gross pay. Net pay is what the employee receives after withholding has been deducted. You are to write checks to the employees for their net pay.
5. After writing all the checks, you are to type a report for management on all employees. Show their name, hours worked, pay rate, gross pay, withholding and net pay, and total all the financial columns.
6. When you finish, sweep the floor.

In this job, you have all the elements of the computer as shown in Figure 2.20.

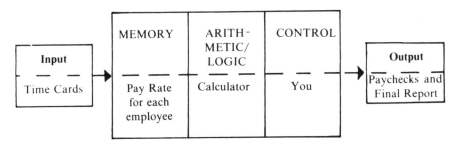

Figure 2.20 *A full computer.*

Figure 2.21 shows a flow chart that describes the entire process. By following the flow chart, a person doing the job as called for, or a computer properly programmed, could always complete the task. The computer can store all the pay rates of all the employees on something like a flexible disk. The name and hours worked can be entered with a keyboard. The computer can also write the

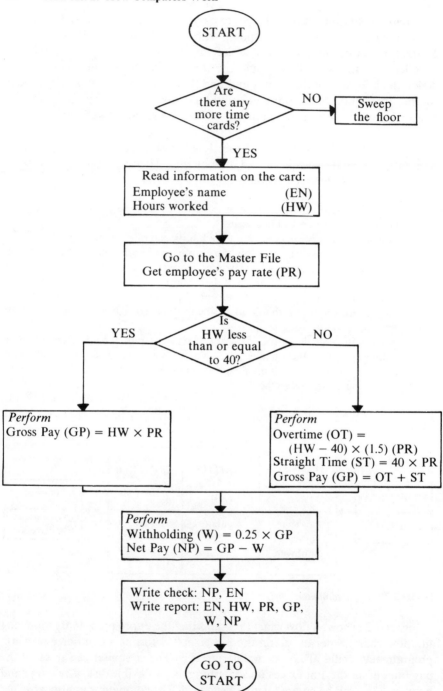

Figure 2.21 *Payroll flow chart.*

checks (as long as the proper forms are loaded into the printer) and then prepare the final report. But it can't sweep the floor.

Business Systems and the Computer

Small businesses, for the most part, have the same anatomy as big businesses. Their "systems"—operations, finance, marketing, and administration—are alike, though the small business has these systems in microcosm. It is important that you, the entrepreneur, keep this in mind as you begin to investigate how various computer systems can aid your business; for a common error at this stage is to underestimate a small business's computer needs.

The "hobby" type of small computer, selling for under $1000, is usually not well suited to small businesses. The reason has to do with **files** of data. Your data files, like the files of a big corporation, break down into two general categories.

- *Master files* that contain relatively permanent information. In our payroll example, the employee's name and pay rate would be contained on a master file. This information would only change when employees change (new hire, resignation, termination) or if their pay rate changes (a raise).
- *Transaction files* that change all the time. In the example, this file would contain the employee's hours worked for any one week. The physical transaction file is usually written over with new information on a periodic basis, just like re-using a dictating cassette.

Often, the transaction and master files may be on the same physical medium (one flexible disk, for example) but it is convenient to have the programs on another one. The very inexpensive computers do not have the capability of dual files, and therefore may make data processing cumbersome. With some of the small machines, you have to load (**read**) the program into the main memory of the machine first and then must have the data ready to be operated on once that procedure has been accomplished. That's pretty slow.

The construction of the files is also important. If both the transaction file and the master file are in random order, processing time will be lengthened because the computer will spend a lot of time searching for things. If both files are in the same order (alphabetical or employee social security number) processing will be a lot faster. Computers can **sort** files all by themselves as long as you tell them what to sort, where that piece of information can be found, and the order to sort it in—ascending or descending.

One other concept of files should be noted. If a file has been constructed in a particular fashion, for example, alphabetically by first name*, that file is said to be *sequential* in nature. If you were to "dump the file" (print everything on it without regard to any changes), it might come out like this:

* You could just as easily have sorted the same file numerically by Zip code.

AAA Distributors
23 Fern St.
Newton MA 02166
    Customer Number: 02166591201

ABC Cleaners
Central Square
Keene NH 03431
    Customer Number: 03431271802

Acme Valve Co.
Main St.
Rutland VT 05401
    Customer Number: 05401365101

and so on. The file is in alphabetical *sequence.*

There may be reasons to select certain things in the file, and therefore it may be necessary to *index* the file. This simply means that a *portion* of the file is to be worked on. Suppose you want to try out the response to a new product or service but only on a test basis. You might select all your customers in Maine and therefore you are interested in all Zip codes from 03900 to 04999. That group is an *index group.* A computer file can be indexed in the same way that you might keep alphabetized 3-by-5 cards on customers.

A final word is in order regarding files and records. You remember that a computer lives with 0's and 1's or bits, and that it usually takes eight bits to make a byte. A byte normally represents one alphabetical character (m, z, a, ?) or two numbers. When enough bytes are assembled to become a recognizable item of data, like a customer name or a date, this collection of data is called a record. When all like records are accumulated, for example all customers, this becomes a file.

Chapter 3 Software

If you were to go into your local computer store and buy the latest model from Electrotron Computers, Ltd., bring it back to your facility, and plug it in, nothing much would happen. Like a hand-held calculator, the computer needs instructions to tell it what to do. These instructions, both the kind that get the machine ready to accept operations like add, subtract, multiply and divide, and those actual operations themselves, are called "software." This distinguishes them from "hardware" (the equipment itself).

Before we get into programming and programming languages, we should define and discuss a few terms that you will hear when standing in a crowd of computerphiles. We will talk about things having to do with systems programs or systems software—translators, interpreters, diagnostics, operating systems, compilers, assemblers—those sets of instructions which get the machine ready to do work for you; tell you when things are wrong; take instructions from a notation that you understand (like $c = a + b$) to a notation that the machine understands (0's and 1's).

Systems Programs

Bootstrap Routine

The term **bootstrap** has pretty much the same connotation in computers as it does in the old saying about lifting oneself up by one's own . . . . After you turn the computer on, you call in the bootstrap program so that all that expensive circuitry can begin to do something besides being a depreciable asset on your balance sheet. You should think about a machine that has internal boot-strap capability by flicking a switch on the panel of the computer and calling the bootstrap program from *inside* the machine. If you ask your computer sales-person about this feature, they will undoubtedly mumble something about **read-only memory (ROM)**. The name denotes exactly what happens inside the circuitry of the machine. There is a section of the computer that has been per-manently designed to hold something like the bootstrap, and, when so in-structed by you, it will "fill up" the circuitry with all the proper instructions to get the machine ready for the next task. The circuitry is called ROM because you can't use that kind of memory—it's permanent, and can only be used by the machine itself on its command. The contents of ROM are usually shifted elec-tronically into the main memory of the computer for further use in processing.

Operating Systems (OS)

The concept of an **operating system (OS)** is sometimes a difficult one for peo-ple who are unfamiliar with a computer. An OS is pure software that helps the machine to operate in its most efficient manner. It does things that you might otherwise have to do yourself. An OS has been likened to the conductor of a symphony orchestra. Each member of the orchestra has a musical score pre-pared for his or her particular instrument and coordinated to be a part of the symphony that will be performed. Without the conductor, the musicians could conceivably begin playing their parts whenever they chose. Although they might be technically correct if considered by themselves, there would be no unity and chaos could result. The OS "orchestrates" the segments of your com-puter into uniform action.

Some small, inexpensive computers do not have operating systems in the true sense of the word. They are simple and basic machines usually consisting of a keyboard, a viewing screen (which can be a home television set), and a basic input/output device such as a cassette tape recorder and/or a floppy disk or two. If such a small machine will not accept a true operating system, it prob-ably does possess some kind of system monitor. Much like software application packages, operating systems are usually purchased separately from the com-puter. (See Chapter 5.) There are a number of OS's available, but one of them has become almost the standard for small computers. It is known as CP/M*, and the initials stand for Control Program/Microcomputer. CP/M has been around for quite a while and there is probably a version specifically designed for the computer which you have in mind. The OS comes on a standard disk-ette (floppy disk) and the system documentation is also supplied in six man-uals; the price is less than $250, and well worth it.

* CP/M is a registered trademark of Digital Research Inc., Box 579, Pacific Grove, CA 93950.

CP/M, like other operating systems, has standard features that come with the package. Some of the features include the ability to:

- Handle entire disk files in an efficient way. Files can be created, named, renamed, read, written, saved, and deleted.
- Transfer information between two devices—cassette tape to floppy disk, for example.
- Edit written text (like a program) quickly and easily.
- Translate high-level languages into machine-understandable language.
- Trace the actual execution of a program as an aid to debugging (finding and fixing errors).
- Determine the status of input/output devices.
- Copy existing files.

OS programs do occupy a piece of your computer's main memory (usually less than 4K), so you will have to make an allowance for that.

If you are buying a computer, ask the salesperson about the operating system: What it does for you, how much it costs, what its limitations are.

Compilers

A **compiler** is a software routine that translates the statements of a "macro" or **high-level language** like **FORTRAN** into a language that the machine can understand (i.e., zeroes and ones). Some compilers are built right into the machine. The program written in FORTRAN is called the **source program**, and the new program, the one created, is known as the **object program**. A compiler reads the entire source program and then converts it *all* to the object module. If you make mistakes compilers can help you, at least with syntax errors. A syntax error, just like an English error, violates the rules of the language—"I gone to the store." Another error, not so easily caught by the compiler, is a logic error, which simply doesn't make sense—"Please hand me the store."

Interpreters

An **interpreter** works like a compiler (in that it changes source to object code), but it only works on one line of program code at one time. The interpreter takes a statement that you have written, translates it, and executes it.

Other Things

There is an entire breed of other software systems that are either built into the machine as a standard feature or are available as options, at extra cost. Be sure of what you're getting and paying for. One thing to look into is the availability of **utility** programs. These are programs which will sort, merge, select, add, delete and so on. (See Chapter 5.)

Programming Languages

Ever since the earliest days of computers, attempts have been made to create languages that both computers and people could easily understand. You know by now that a computer gets its jollies with 1's (a signal or voltage present) and 0's (no signal). Therefore, you might logically conclude that one way to program a computer is to give it a diet of 101001111010001100 . . . etc. True, but boring. And it takes forever just to tell the machine to add two numbers together. Although simplified, the binary instructions to add two one-digit numbers together (2 and 5, for example) would go something like this:

1. Clear register 1
2. Clear register 2
3. Clear accumulator
4. Enter a 2 (10) on the keyboard
5. Load in register 1, clear keyboard
6. Load a 5 (101) on the keyboard
7. Load in register 2, clear keyboard
8. Move contents of register 1 to accumulator
9. Clear register 1
10. Add contents of register 2 to contents of accumulator
11. Clear register 2
12. Move contents of accumulator to register 1
13. Clear accumulator
14. Move contents of register 1 to printer
15. Print

What a mess, right? And the whole thing would be in 0's and 1's.

Along came **assembly language** to save scientists from Bellevue. Assembly language allowed people to say things which might resemble something like,

00024   ADD   00418   01017

which might mean:

Take the contents of location 24, add it to the contents of location 418 and put the result in location 1017.

Still pretty bulky.

So FORTRAN was developed, along with JOVIAL, PL/1, **COBOL**, AL-GOL, RPG, SIMSCRIPT, APL, **BASIC**, and others.

FORTRAN

FORTRAN has one basic problem: It is a scientific language. Engineers love it; business people hate it. It has severe limitations in handling lots of data. You have to be very careful when using numbers, like the Zip code, that don't have an implied decimal point.

A typical FORTRAN statement would be

IF (X . GTE . (Y − 6.2)) GO TO 12

which comes out "if some value of X is greater than or equal to some value of Y minus 6.2, then branch off to statement number 12, otherwise keep going." The chances of your ever seeing FORTRAN as the language for a computer in a small business are slim.

BASIC

Beginner's All-purpose Symbolic Instruction Code, an offshoot of FOR-TRAN, was developed at Dartmouth College in 1964 by John Kemeny and Thomas Kurtz. The major advantages of BASIC are that it is simple, and it is *interactive.* An interactive language is one that permits two-way communication between computer and operator—the computer can prompt you or ask you questions if it is programmed for an interactive language. BASIC is still somewhat mathematical in its structure, but most people have been able to learn it fairly well.

We highly recommend that you consider a machine that will accept BASIC. It has apparently become *the* language of the smaller computers, and will continue to dominate the field.*

Programming in BASIC. It is not the purpose of this book to teach you how to program a computer in the BASIC language. Any good-sized bookstore will have a paperback selling for under $10 that will do this job. Learning BASIC takes an actual computer so that you can see your mistakes, learn from them, and get to be a pretty respectable programmer yourself. Don't be scared and don't be intimidated. Anyone can learn to program a computer. *Anyone.*

* By the way, there is no one standard BASIC language—there are versions within versions. There is one language called **CBASIC** (Commercial BASIC) and even that has different levels or versions. Don't be alarmed. The versions are not that different from one another.

Though it is not our aim to teach BASIC, the discussion of this most common small business computer language is a good place at which to describe briefly how performing computer operations in BASIC works.

To program in BASIC you normally sit in front of some kind of terminal that has a keyboard. Your particular small computer will, at the outset, have you do a few things to get the machine ready to accept a program, like type some identification into the machine, hit some sequence of command keys, or tell the machine what time it is.

In BASIC, as in FORTRAN, the symbols used for the four common mathematical functions are

+   add

−   subtract

*   multiply

/   divide

Therefore the expression (8 + 2)/5 would result in the eight and the two being added together to produce ten, which would then be divided by five. Note the use of the set of parentheses. If we wanted to see the actual answer, we could write

PRINT   (8 + 2)/5

and "2" would be displayed on the CRT. Let's write a program to do this problem and display the answer.

Every command needs a statement number (from 1 to 9999, usually) and the most common convention is to increment each succeeding statement by ten. Some computers will do this automatically. Here is our program:

0010   LET A = 8

0020   LET B = 2

0030   LET C = 5

0040   LET D = (A + B)/C

0050   PRINT D

0060   END

The word "LET" assigns a value to a variable. Note the use of the word "END" in statement 0060; this tells the computer that it has reached the end of the program.

When you hit the button marked "RUN" (or type in the command), the screen of your terminal will show:

RUN

2

END AT 0060

The "2" is the answer and the last statement shows where the computer stopped in the program.

With BASIC you can write your name:

0110   PRINT "J. PIERPONT MORGAN"

call in data from some other place:

0070   INPUT A

or skip around the program:

1210   GO TO 0080

See if you can figure out what is happening in the following program:

```
0010        READ N

0020        PRINT N;

0030        READ H, W

0040        LET S = H * W

0050        PRINT H; "HRS"; W; "/HR"; S; "SALARY"

0060        DATA 14017, 40, 5.25

0070        END
```

It's the old wage-rate thing, isn't it? Commas (,) separate unique items and semicolons (;) tell the computer to leave a full space between items when printing. What happens in the wage program?

0010   The computer is told to read a variable called N. But where is N? It's the first variable in the DATA statement, number 0060. So the computer knows that N is equal to 14017 and any time that N is used, it will have the value 14017 (the employee number).

0020   The computer is told to write the value for N on the next available line.

0030   It now picks up a value of 40 for H (hours) and 5.25 for W (hourly wage).

0040   Computation of a new variable, S (salary), which is H times W or 40 $\times$ 5.25 = 210.00

0050   Answers and writing are displayed. Including the value for N already written, the entire line would be:

14017   40 HRS   5.25 /HR   210.00 SALARY

If you can follow all that is going on, you are well on your way to becoming a real programmer.

COBOL (COmmon Business-Oriented Language)

The chances of your running into COBOL with small computers are increasing. If the machine that you are looking at has COBOL only, or a doctored version of it like Digital Equipment Corporation's DIBOL, remember that COBOL is a "programmer's" language. It often takes a year or more to become skilled in its use. Still, COBOL is learnable just as BASIC is learnable.

COBOL came out around 1959 as an answer to business programmers' hatred for FORTRAN. COBOL is very good at handling large files of information, shuffling them around with a minimum of calculation, and then writing out other large files. FORTRAN (and BASIC) are better suited to smaller amounts of input and output data, but are able to perform many intricate calculations.

A COBOL program normally contains four "Divisions" that can be broken down into sections.

Identification Division. The first part does not contain any information that will be operated on. It simply supplies basic data and may look like:

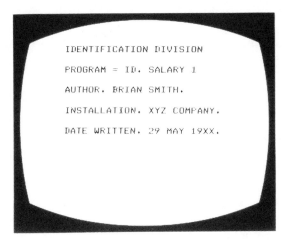

```
IDENTIFICATION DIVISION

PROGRAM = ID. SALARY 1

AUTHOR. BRIAN SMITH.

INSTALLATION. XYZ COMPANY.

DATE WRITTEN. 29 MAY 19XX.
```

Environment Division. Although this division can get rather complicated, its main purpose is to spell out the particulars about the computer (type, size), to define the input/output equipment, and to specify some things about the various files and records.

Data Division. This part, which can have two or three sections, describes the variables that will be used in the program. Before we could use a variable, such as an employee number, we would have to say:

$$01 \quad N \quad PICTURE \quad 9(5)$$

The computer would then know that the employee number, N, is always a five-digit number—hence the "9."

Procedure Division. It is here that the actual computation is done. Each COBOL statement begins with a verb:

MULTIPLY HOURS BY WAGE GIVING SALARY

COBOL can get complex, but some of the newer, interactive COBOL is pretty simple. Don't rule a computer out of the running because it only has COBOL, just know what you're getting into before you write a check for $20,000 or so. The use of COBOL in business computers will probably increase. Some of the newer computers can handle both BASIC AND COBOL.

PASCAL

This language, named for seventeenth-century French philosopher and mathematician Blaise Pascal, was developed in Switzerland in the late 1960's and has become firmly established in our nation's colleges and universities as a teaching language. PASCAL is easy to learn and studies have shown that students who become proficient in it have no difficulty learning other languages such as COBOL or BASIC. One major benefit of PASCAL is that it practically forces a programmer to follow a predetermined, logical sequence of steps in preparing a program. This means a major reduction in the number of errors. If any language stands a chance of having a significant future impact on small business data processing, it is PASCAL.

PL/1

PL/1 was originally intended as a replacement for both FORTRAN and COBOL. Until recently, there were few effective compilers available that would allow PL/1 to be run on small computers. Although the language is easy to learn and is modular in its structure (programs can be written in pieces rather than all at once), it is doubtful that it will have any major impact in small business.

C

That's right—the letter "C." It was used by the telephone company for many years and has now appeared on a few small computers, notably those of Digital Equipment Corporation. It is a complex language, in that a programmer must learn quite a bit about the hardware that is being used if he is to employ C. Unlike BASIC, there is only one standard version of C. Its acceptance in small business computing is highly unlikely.

Chapter 4 The Coming of the Computer in Small Business

I happened to be reading a book by John Kemeny, president of Dartmouth College (and one of the developers of BASIC), entitled *Man and the Computer* (Charles Scribner's Sons, New York). The book was published in 1972, which means that it was probably written in 1970. The following is a direct quotation from page 122:

> We may assume that by 1990 *even* [emphasis added] a small business will have its own terminal.

Even a mind as seminal as Kemeny's missed two things in this prediction: the year and the level of equipment. A decade before 1990, small businesses don't even bother with terminals—they use the computer itself!

As I am putting these words on paper, they are being outdated. With that warning in mind, I am going to "borrow" the remainder of this chapter from a good friend and former student, Bob Vitelli. In the summer of 1979, Bob conducted a study of small business and the computer. The study became the subject of his senior thesis at Franklin Pierce College, and one of the best done in the school's history.

The study, as I have adapted it for this chapter, speaks for itself, sometimes in its author's words, and sometimes in ours.

Small Business Systems

The manufacture of small business systems and minicomputers has experienced phenomenal growth over the past few years. Minicomputers surged 38 percent to $3.2 billion, and small business systems climbed 30 percent to $1.6 billion in fiscal year 1978, according to estimates by International Data Corporation.*

The fastest growing information-processing market for the 1980's and beyond will be small business systems. Sales are expected to increase by around 40 percent over the decade. During the past several years, almost every traditional large-scale computer manufacturer has entered the small business marketplace. The cause for this switch from a relatively conservative position to such a major commitment is expressed by Martin R. Durbec of Sperry Univac. He suggests, "The main reason the large computer companies have entered the small business systems marketplace after virtually ignoring it for many years is that small business computer sales are growing at a considerably faster rate than sales of larger computers, and promise to do so for the foreseeable future." †

The Small Business Computer Market

During the past few years major developments have occurred within the computer industry. Many new companies have formed for the purpose of manufacturing small business computer systems, hardware, and software, and a large potential market for computer systems has emerged.

Small business firms constitute an important part of today's business system. Owners and managers of small business enterprises must be able to anticipate and adjust quickly to the ever-changing shifts in consumer demand and competition. With double-digit inflation affecting businesses across the nation, the need for the small business entrepreneur to be cost-conscious and aware of the business environment is of major importance. There has been concern over the coming recession and the slowdowns in the economy that a recession inevitably causes. The small businessman, caught between rising costs and lower profit margins, may find that his survival is dependent on his ability to make quick, educated decisions regarding his business concerns. Whereas before he could only dream of computerizing, the time has finally arrived where it is possible

---

* "Computers: High Growth That Goes On and On," *Business Week,* Jan. 8, 1979, p. 39.
† Martin R. Durbec, "Choosing Computers: Now It's Your Turn," *Small Business Computers Magazine,* May 1978, p. 18.

for the entrepreneur, in most cases, to purchase at a reasonable price a computer system designed specifically for his needs.

That the computer industry has realized the importance and potential of the small business market is obvious. What needs further clarification is how small businesses use, view, and accept the new computer technology which has been made available to them. Furthermore, as this study was exploratory in nature, the answer to this question should help locate potential problem areas and help build a base for more extensive research in the future.

Need for Computer Education in Small Business

The owners of a number of small businesses in the Northeast were asked about their views on having a computer as a part of their operation. Most of these businesses did not have a computer, nor did they use an outside computer service bureau for any extensive data processing. A few ventures had payroll checks prepared by their banks. To summarize the results of the study:

- The major problem was education. In the majority of cases, owners were unfamiliar with the computer industry, systems, and applications. Misconceptions and half-truths were the rule rather than the exception. Some owners stated that salespeople from computer manufacturers had stopped by, but that their visits were not of sufficient length to help.
- A majority of those owners contacted simply couldn't see how a computer would help them. This response is closely linked to a lack of knowledge, but also stems from a failure on their part to recognize or admit to problem areas in the business.
- More than 50 percent of those interviewed said that computers were beyond their financial reach. They said this without being able to relate to the benefits and potential cost saving available with a computer.
- A significant number of entrepreneurs viewed the computer with fear and would not welcome a change in their ways of doing business.
- Some owners were under the impression that they would have to hire "computer people" if they were to purchase a machine.

The entire Vitelli study pointed to the need for knowledge and information. In many cases, either the information that business owners had about computers was insufficient, or it was misleading, or both. This book is a direct result of Robert Vitelli's study. It was written to dispel some of the myths that the study found business owners have about computers, and to provide some basic knowledge so that intelligent questions can be posed by business owners before a decision on whether or not to take on a computer is reached.

Summary

By 1990, the year in which John Kemeny predicted that use of the computer would have penetrated to the level of small business, most small businesses will have some form of computer support. Most, indeed, will own their own equipment.

Speed and accuracy, the two critical advantages that the computer brought to big business, are what will win it its commanding place in small business, as well. The amount of information handled in small businesses today exceeds the capacity of the entrepreneur to order it, understand it, and put it to use. The "response time" of normal business operations and conditions must be reduced if a business owner is to keep the business under control as well as competitive. Not only must information be handled in **real time** (that is, today, not next week), but demands for precision and detail have increased as well. The computer can provide for both these needs, increasing profitability.

Chapter 5, on computer applications, will give you a better feel for the ways a computer can take on various tasks in a small business. Chapter 6 will guide you in determining whether the expenses and other demands of a computer are justified in your own enterprise.

Chapter 5 Applications

Your new computer will be nothing more than a very impressive piece of machinery until you get it to work for you, in application to your own business situation. This stark fact will introduce the notion of **applications software,** for it is through software, or programs, that your computer will be made to serve you. This chapter is intended not so much to teach you specific tasks that you can do with your computer; rather, it is intended to indicate ways to approach the entire subject of applications software.

Beyond the initial price of your computer hardware and supplies, you will have a major investment in software—either **package software** (finished programs all ready to run on your machine), or **custom software** (prepared uniquely for your machine), or a mix of the two (a prepared program that is adapted to your particular business).*

Small computer hardware systems are selling like wild. In Chapter 4 we projected that small business systems will grow at about 40 percent through the 1980's. Hundreds of hardware manufacturers are competing in what has become a massive market. Some companies, like IBM, Digital Equipment Corporation, and Data General Corporation (DGC), offer not only complete computer systems with a nearly infinite number of configurations, options, and

---

* About the best overall estimate for planning purposes is that the software should run about 30 percent of the cost of the hardware. That is a "one-time" cost, not the cost of maintaining and changing the software.

45

add-ons; they also offer entire lines of computer systems within the same general model series: from small, basic machines costing several thousand dollars to the big brothers and sisters of the family that go well over $100,000.

The software end of the business, although nowhere nearly as large, is growing more rapidly than the hardware end. This is because it is relatively easy for a company—or even one person—to get into the programming business, whereas to enter the hardware business might require a large amount of capital and a heavy investment in engineering and design, as well as marketing.

Don't get caught in the trap of thinking only about the physical hardware of your computer. In these times, it is important that you think about your business first, and that usually means software. Too many entrepreneurs rush to buy a machine and then face the How-do-I-use-it? problem. That's backwards. Hardware is important, to be sure, but it is not as important as the software.

Most similarly priced computers are comparable in what they can do. It's true that Company A's $20,000 machine may be able to access a given piece of data one-thousandth of a second faster than Company B's $20,000 machine, or may be superior in some other such trivial matter; but they all operate in essentially the same manner unless they are special-purpose computers, such as those designed for use in an accountant's office. The machines that you look at in any general-purpose category will be so much alike that you shouldn't spend a lot of time getting concerned over internal operation and specifications. The backup that the manufacturer offers in terms of service, and his reputation among small businesses, are much more important.

Most small computers today are reliable machines that require very little maintenance compared to their early cousins. Unless you get an electronic lemon, you will not be spending much time fussing with keeping the hardware operating. Instead, your time (or someone else's) will be spent with software— getting it to run correctly, discovering **bugs** and fixing them, adding new twists to the program, and keeping existing programs up to date. Federal, state, and even local governments (there are a total of 80,000 in the U.S.) are constantly diddling around with tax withholding rates and even your simplest payroll program will have to be changed at the whim of these bureaucracies.

Finding Appropriate Software

Real experts in the small business computer field understand small business first and computers second. This is the classic—and classically misguided—way that many business owners have gotten into computers. The pattern is as follows:

1. Buy the computer.
2. Buy or write some software.
3. Try to shoehorn both the hardware and the software to fit the business.

With that approach, no wonder there are a lot of disillusioned people around. The right way to proceed is to

1. Define what it is within the business that needs automating.
2. Find the software that will do that.
3. Buy a machine that will run the software.

This is the way that will result in the best system for your business. Too many people start looking for a machine with no real idea of what it is that they want the computer to do for them. They fall prey to some slick salesperson who snows them with stuff about **bytes** and **bauds** (bits per second), are paralyzed into not asking the right questions, and wind up with a machine that they feel obligated to find work for.

Before you seriously talk about any part of a computer, you need to examine your business from a transaction standpoint. What activities make up the business day? The more time you spend on this analysis in the beginning, the better the decisions that you will make later. We do not intend in this book to give you a method of analysis for your business, but we will offer a few suggestions. You should be able to explain to a computer vendor what you want the computer to do for you. This will save a lot of time (and possibly money as well) and you will wind up with a machine and software that is better suited to you and your operation.

Your Business

Your business is both standard and unique at the same time. It is standard from the viewpoint that your business receives and disburses cash—it is a money machine in the final analysis. Chances are that if your business is a gift store, you run the operation pretty much like every other gift shop. There is a fair degree of latitude in the phrase "pretty much" because some part of the business is unique. There is some part of the business that you run quite differently from every other gift store in the world. Therefore, you need to know how much of your business is standard so that you can use prepared software programs as much as possible, but at the same time you need to be aware of how much of the business is unique.

Even if you never buy a computer, it will be extremely helpful to you to analyze the various "systems" within your business. You may find out some very interesting things as a result. To help you in assessing data processing and how it can aid your business, it will be necessary to write down a few things.

Take each and every functional area within your business and label it. Although each area or potential application will be different for different businesses, such a list might include:

- receipts and disbursements
- accounts receivable and billing
- accounts payable
- inventory control
- budgeting
- customer mailing list
- payroll

For each of these potential applications, it is important to know the number and size of the transactions that take place over a given span of time. For instance, an account payable is created each time you receive a good or a service and do not pay for that good or service at time of receipt. As a part of the analysis, you should also know how many records will be created as a result of one account receivable. If you don't know exactly, estimate what it is and then double that estimate. Record size is important because all computers have a limit to their memory size and you don't want to run out of capacity early in the game.

As a very simple example of estimating sizes, assume that you want to analyze your payroll system. Most computer vendors will help you with this since they have the forms all ready and have done this many times, but it's important for you to understand the process so that you can relate the potential sizes of your files to external memory devices like floppy and hard disks, and therefore to the hardware that you need, and thence to what all this will cost. Many small-business owners have found themselves severely limited when it came to external memory and now wish that they had either gone for more capacity or waited for the hard disk to come along for small computers.

In doing this example, we will assume that a small business has 15 employees who are paid weekly. There will be two files with which the business owner must be concerned: the employee file, that gives basic information about each person; and the check file, that holds the information the business owner will need to retain for record-keeping purposes. There may be some added disk space required, but we will take care of that at the end of the calculations.

Employee File

This file contains information about the employees and their rate and frequency of pay, and is used to prepare paychecks. The table below shows some elements that might be contained in such a file and the maximum number of characters that would be allowed for each of the records:

Item	*Maximum Record Length (characters)*
1. Employee name	25
2. Street address	25
3. City	20

4. State	2
5. Zip code	5
6. Social security number	9
7. Number of dependents	2
8. Rate of pay	6
9. Frequency of pay	2
10. Various codes for deductions (bonds, insurance)	20
11. Miscellaneous codes	20
12. Total	136 characters

Check File

This file is essentially an image of the check and the check stub that is produced for the employee:

Item	Maximum Record Length (characters)
1. Name (payee)	25
2. Social security number	9
3. Check number	5
4. Date of check	6
5. Amount of check (net pay)	8
6. Gross pay	8
7. Federal income tax	8
8. State income tax	8
9. FICA	8
10. Period worked	6
11. Miscellaneous codes	20
12. Total	111 characters

Summary

Employee file (15 employees × 136 characters)	2,040 characters
Check file	
(52 weeks × 15 employees × 111 characters)	86,580 characters

We will concern ourselves with the check file, since it is by far the largest. The size of 86,580 characters will be the absolute minimum, since employees may be replaced or new employees hired, which will necessitate adding new information. The best rule is simply to double the count to 173,160 characters. If the owner of this business is looking at a floppy disk capable of storing 300K characters, there would be plenty of room for an entire year's transactions.

In addition to estimating record size, you should have an idea of the kinds of reports that you want for each application. We will give you some help later in this chapter and the programs that are available will also have ideas for you, but you should decide what you need first. Maybe what you want is not immediately feasible but at least you will start from the standpoint of what you want rather than be forced to adapt your operation to the first thing that you see.

As you are going through your thinking, keep one eye on the future. You may have 1000 different items in your inventory now, but by next year that figure may jump to 2000 or 5000. One business owner made a decision to take on a new dealership in automotive parts just after the purchase of a small computer. The initial stocking order overflowed the machine. Since the computer that they had purchased could not be expanded, the owner had to buy a newer, larger machine and then wound up with a very expensive, slightly used toy for the kids.

With your "want" list of potential computer applications in your hands, you are in a much better position to talk with computer vendors. You want a machine that will work for you, and they want to sell computer hardware and software systems. You'll be more confident about what you know best—your business—and the salesperson won't have to spend a lot of time asking questions. It will bring both of you to your common goal more quickly, probably less expensively, and with a minimum of hassle and possible future problems.

If you have already begun your search for a computer, you undoubtedly have come across an interesting paradox—the people who make the physical machine don't usually supply the applications software to go with it. This is true even for many larger manufacturers. Hardware companies are good at hardware, but usually not so good on software. Normally, a hardware company will recommend two or three software houses who produce applications for the machines in question. This is one reason why we suggest that, after doing some thinking about your business transactions, you go to someone who can talk with you about software. A good place to visit in this regard is your friendly neighborhood computer retail store. Rick Fortin of Compu'Center in Wellesley, Massachusetts, recently talked about how a "typical" visit by a small-business owner would go at his facility. He mentioned that gross sales are not a good indicator of the nature of computer needs; the type of business is much more important. Mr. Fortin sees the interplay between himself and the entrepreneur as having four separate phases:

- *Discovery.* The entrepreneur is asked to explain the various methods and procedures within his or her business and the overall nature of the business itself. The question that Mr. Fortin wants answered in detail is, "How are you now doing business?" The final hardware/software combination depends on the number and complexity of the transactions in the particular business. He also wants to know about both the administrative organization (departmentalized, subsidiary companies) and the physical setup, especially if there are remote locations. One question that he asks is why the owner wants a computer. The most common response is that a computer can keep track of the business's operation. Mr. Fortin's next question has to do with the entrepreneur's ability to change his business methods. If he sees his business as being in trouble from a lack of correct information, the chances are that a computer will only get him more deeply in trouble, at a faster rate. If the owner says that the business systems "can't" be changed, he is sent on his way with some friendly advice. Some change will be required.

- *Education.* Mr. Fortin takes the approach that most small-business owners don't need to know how a computer works, only what it can do, so he explains the machine in the same way that any other salesperson would explain a technical product like a television set or a car. He stays away from most of the esoteric stuff and discusses the benefits a computer offers. Using what he has found out about the owner's business and its needs for data processing, he will mention price *ranges*—usually brought up by the prospective buyer at some point anyway. The price categories that Mr. Fortin uses include both hardware and software and are meant to be ballpark figures: *Level 1–$20,000.* The basic machine consisting of a CPU, a CRT/Keyboard, and a couple of floppy disks; *Level 2–$30,000.* A slightly larger version of Level 1, with the addition of a hard disk or two; *Level 3–$40,000.* Multiple terminals, multiple hard disks, communications capability, ability of the CPU to work on more than one task at a time.
- *Demonstration.* The demonstration phase usually consists of selecting some sample piece of software—for example, an accounts receivable package—and having the software run on two or more different machines. The business owner can see the different speeds and procedures of the equipment in operation. Usually Mr. Fortin will show the difference in performance between floppy disks and hard disks as well.
- *Sale.* This phase is open-ended, depending upon how everything progresses. Few sales take place immediately. There is often quite a bit of education still left to do. In many instances, the business owner wants to visit an installation of the machine or machines that he or she is interested in to learn more about how they operate in an actual small business environment.

Buying Software

You will discover that there are four different ways to approach software. These approaches are outlined briefly in the following paragraphs.

Turnkey Software

A **turnkey** software system is just what the name implies: to get everything ready to go, all you do is turn the key. (Many computers actually have a lock on the front panel which supplies power to the machine.) The programs are essentially all part of the computer itself. Turnkey systems are not very popular in small business because of their inflexibility. Your business will change and you want the ability to change your processing as well. Many turnkey programs can be changed only by the manufacturer, and then only at a high cost. This is also called a **dedicated** system since it is dedicated to only one or several very specific applications. Turnkey systems are available for professionals like lawyers (for billing and time recording) and CPA's (for client accounting procedures).

Be very leery of anyone trying to sell you either a turnkey or a dedicated system. Someday there may be a perfect machine/software combination that will solve all your problems, but such a breakthrough at the present time is highly unlikely.

Packaged (Canned) Software

The package software approach is by far the most popular. Normally, when small-business owners purchase a computer, they also purchase software to go with it if they want to get the machine up and running in a minimum amount of time. The "package" consists of the program itself, already recorded on some such medium as a floppy disk, and some printed documentation to support the program. One thing you must be certain about: *Be sure that the application you buy will run on your machine!* Many new computer owners have purchased a program that will not operate on the computer that they own. They may own the proper machine model, but their internal memory may not be large enough or they may not have double-sided double-density floppy disks or whatever else is required. A retail computer store will help you to select the software that will do your job and that will work on your machine. If you buy the applications yourself through the mail or by telephone, be certain that you are buying something that will work.

Purchase prices for packaged software vary from a few dollars for very simple programs (like one to record your checkbook transactions) to over $10,000 for complex systems. Some experts in the field tell small-business owners to estimate a cost of $1000 per major application (accounts receivable, etc.)

Unless you are one business in one hundred you will find that the package application you have purchased won't fit your operation 100 percent. For example, the field that you use to describe an inventory item may be larger than the program will allow—you use 35 alphanumeric characters and the program has a limitation of 25 characters. Another common example is that a business owner may want a particular report that a canned program does not provide. For a variety of reasons, then, the program will have to be modified in one way or another. You can have this done by someone outside your company or it can be done internally.

Outside. Using people outside of your company means that you will probably pay an hourly rate—in some cases up to $75 per hour. If you buy a package from a computer dealer, as opposed to doing it by mail, usually the dealer has the capability to make the modifications and may have done something similar for another business. The dealer is usually licensed by the company that originally developed the software to sell the software package, to make modifications to the package for the user, and to maintain the package with scheduled modifications and updates that are released from time to time by the firm that wrote the program. Some entrepreneurs bring in "moonlighters" to make adaptations to a purchased program. These part-timers may be teachers, programmers working a regular job, hobbyists, salespeople—anyone who has gained basic programming knowledge. New computer owners may feel that they are saving a lot of money by having someone come in during the evening at $10–$15 per hour. However, there are a number of potential problems that may occur as a result of this attempt to save money:

- The person doing the modification may have to spend several hours, or even days, becoming familiar with the computer, the program or both. The business owner winds up paying for this learning period.
- There is no assurance that the person doing the work is skilled at making these modifications.
- The part-timer has nothing to gain from the relationship except money.
- The software firm may void any guarantees as a result of unauthorized persons tinkering with the program.

Internally. Maybe the adaptations you want can be done by you or by one of your people. Computers today are wonderful, self-teaching tools. You can buy almost any machine that sells for less than $15,000, get a $5 or $10 book on COBOL or BASIC programming, and start to write some simple routines in an hour or two. As with learning any new skill, practice and time will improve your technique, but don't start tackling a job like modifying an existing program. This would be like buying a piano and attempting to restructure a Chopin étude before you have learned a scale. Some of the newer programs, however, help or prompt you to change various items.

Our recommendation is to work closely with a reputable dealer who sells both hardware and software (preferably three or more nationally known brands of each). Most dealer sales personnel understand both small business and computer systems, and can also afford to spend more time with you than many salespeople who work directly for large computer manufacturers can. Talk with some other small-business owners who have computers already to get insights on whom to deal with—and not to deal with.

Learn-By-Doing (With Help)

There is a mixed approach available that is a do-it-yourself solution. You purchase a software "kit" for $50 or so which includes a guide to writing a program for a specific application (inventory, for example) as well as an explanation of what is going on. Some books give actual lines of programming code. The major drawback with this workbook approach is that it does require some computer expertise, as the books are usually written for programmers. On the other hand, the cost is minimal. If you went this way and it didn't work, there would be no great financial loss. Again, find someone who has tried this approach in the past—preferably someone who started with your current level of expertise.

The company that has pioneered in applications workbooks is

Osborne Associates/McGraw-Hill Co.
630 Bancroft Way
Berkeley, CA 94710

If you write to them in care of their marketing department, they will furnish you with basic introductory information as well as the name of your nearest dealer. Most Osborne dealers can prepare ready-to-run disks directly from the books, which provide operator instructions and the other necessary documentation. Figure 5.1 shows sample pages of their material to give you some idea of how their books are set up.

Figure 5.1 *From* Accounts Payable and Accounts Receivable—CBASIC *by Lon Poole, Mary Borchers, Martin McNiff, Robert Thompson. Copyright 1979 by McGraw-Hill, Inc. Used with permission of Osborne/McGraw-Hill.*

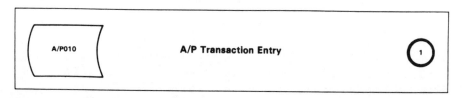

PURPOSE: **Enter new invoices, debit and credit memos, and delete or modify existing invoices.**

WHEN: **Daily or as needed.**

TO EXIT: **Enter an operation code of '0'.**

All new Accounts Payable transactions are entered using this program. They may be entered as invoices, credit memos or debit memos. These newly entered transactions remain on the Transaction file until Update is run, when they are recorded permanently on the Invoice file.

The first step toward changing a transaction which has already been updated to the Invoice file is made using this program. Enter a MODIFY or DELETE transaction for the existing Invoice file record; when Update is run, the modify or delete transaction affects the more permanent Invoice file record.

If you have calculated and paid an invoice by hand, you should still enter the information on the computer. First, write the check information onto your most recent Check Register report (see Report 6-1, page 106), making sure to assign a Check Register number. Then, if the invoice has been entered onto the computer as an unpaid invoice, enter the Check Register number (and Check Date, if desired) for the invoice using the MODIFY operation; entering the Check Register number marks the invoice as "paid", and the Job, General Ledger and Vendor files will be updated accordingly. It also serves as a safety check against paying this invoice twice, since you could pay it again using the computer if it isn't flagged as "paid". If the invoice has not yet been entered onto the computer, enter the invoice information as a NEW INVOICE or DEBIT MEMO, making sure to enter the Check Register number at the same time; the Job, General Ledger and Vendor files will then be updated to include the information from this invoice.

Partial payments of invoices and debit memos are possible, but involve a fairly elaborate procedure. We suggest the following method for making partial payments, but you may devise a method better suited for your use. Initially, modify the existing invoice amount to the amount left to be paid after the desired partial payment is made (you will have to subtract to find the balance due yourself). For example, if you have an invoice for $2000 and want to pay $900, you would modify the $2000 amount to $1100. Then create a new invoice or debit memo for the amount to be paid. We suggest you assign this new invoice an invoice number close to the original invoice number, such as 5222 for an original invoice number of 5221. All other invoice field information should be similar to the original invoice, except the description (field 2), which you may want to enter as a reference to the original invoice number. Then, in Check Calculate, pay off the new invoice (your desired partial payment). See Chapter 3 for more discussion on this procedure.

Partial use of credit memos is calculated automatically, so there is no need for any elaborate transaction entry as there is for partial payment of invoices and debit memos.

Before entering any daily transactions you should remember to change Today's Date in General Information File Maintenance.

SELECT OPERATION

A/P TRANSACTION ENTRY
OPERATION: 0=EXIT; 1=NEW INV; 2=DEL; 3=MOD; 4=CREDIT; 5=DEBIT

1) **Enter operation code** (0-5).

   0 - EXIT. Program ends. The Menu is loaded.

   1 - NEW INVOICE. Request to enter a new invoice; proceed to step 2.

   2 - DELETE. Request to delete an Invoice file record; proceed to step 2.

   3 - MODIFY. Request to change an Invoice file record; proceed to step 2.

   4 - CREDIT MEMO. Request to enter a new credit memo; proceed to step 2.

   5 - DEBIT MEMO. Request to enter a new debit memo; proceed to step 2.

SELECT VENDOR

VENDOR   xxxxxx

2) **Enter vendor number** (0-6 characters).

   ⌐ **— Transaction entry for this vendor and operation is complete.** A new operation is requested; return to step 1.

   Vendor number - Request to enter a transaction for this vendor. A check is made to see if the requested vendor is on the Vendor file:

   If yes, the vendor name and address are displayed as shown in CRT 1-1. You may proceed with the requested operation:

   If NEW INVOICE, CREDIT MEMO or DEBIT MEMO, proceed to step 3.

   If DELETE or MODIFY, proceed to step 4.

   If no, the bulletin NOT ON FILE is flashed. The vendor must be on the Vendor file before a transaction may be entered for that vendor (use Vendor File Maintenance). A new vendor number is requested; repeat this step.

Figure 5.1 *Cont.*

CRT 1-1

```
 _____
/                                                              \
|                                                               |
|   A/P  TRANSACTION  ENTRY                                      |
|                                                               |
|                                                               |
|   <bulletin>                                                  |
|   VENDOR      dddddd                                          |
|   INVOICE     xxxxxx                                          |
|                       dddddddddddddddddddddddddd              |
|                       dddddddddddddddddddddddddd              |
|                       dddddddddddddddddddddddddd              |
|                       dddddddddddddddddddddddddd              |
|                                                               |
|                                                               |
|                                                               |
|                                                               |
|                                                               |
_____/
```

d = display only,   x = enter only,   z = enter or display with option to change

SELECT INVOICE (NEW INVOICE, CREDIT MEMO, DEBIT MEMO)

When entering a new A/P transaction, you must assign a unique invoice, credit memo or debit memo number to each (referred to collectively as invoice numbers). **If possible, assign invoice and debit memo numbers in the range 1-989999, and confine credit memo numbers to the 990000-999999 range.** This method of assigning invoice numbers ensures that, during check calculation, the maximum amount of any credit memo will be applied toward payment of invoices and debit memos.

INVOICE # xxxxxx

3) Enter invoice number (0-999999).

0 - Entry for this vendor and/or operation complete. A new vendor is requested; return to step 2.

Invoice number - Request to create an Invoice record with this number for this vendor. A check is made to see if a record with this invoice number already exists for this vendor on the Invoice file:

If yes, the bulletin ALREADY ON FILE is flashed. A new invoice number is requested; repeat this step.

If no, you may proceed with the requested operation:

If NEW INVOICE or DEBIT MEMO, proceed to step 5.

If CREDIT MEMO, proceed to step 7.

Figure 5.1 *Cont.*

```
        DATA "INVOICE", " ", " ", "CR MEMO", "DB MEMO", "NEW", "DELETE", \
        "MODIFY"
        RESTORE
        FOR I%=1 TO 8: READ A3S(I%): NEXT I%
        MASKA$=" #####.##"
        MASKB$="#####.##"
        MASKC$="#####.#    ######.##"
        MASKD$=" #####.#    ######.##      ######.##"
        MASKD$=##                 ######.##
        DEF FNR(Z9)=(INT(ABS(Z9)*100+.5)/100)*SGN(Z9)      REMARK   ROUND TO NEAREST CENT
        DEF FND(Z9)=FNR(Z9)*SGN(D2)                        REMARK   USED IN G/L & JOB POSTING AMOUNT VERIFICATIONS
10.60   RETURN
.314    RETURN

%INCLUDE SUBS1
%INCLUDE BINSEAFC                                          REMARK   THIS SPACE FOR G/L BINARY SEARCH ROUTINE
%INCLUDE READINV                                          REMARK   THIS SPACE FOR G/L EXTENT INFORMATION READ ROUTINE
%INCLUDE WRITEINV
%INCLUDE READVEND
%INCLUDE A/P-INFO

5000    PPINT CLEAR-SCREENS; "A/P TRANSACTION ENTRY"
        RETURN

5010    IF F=0 OR F>9 THEN GOTO 5040                       REMARK   BRANCH TO ENTER DATA IN FIELD "F"
        ON F GOTO 5040,5050,5060,5070,5080,5090,5100,5110,5120

5040    X1=462:X2=8:X3=0:X4=0:GOSUB 345                    REMARK   ENTER PURCHASE ORDER NO.
        W2S=X0S
        RETURN

5050    X1=526:X2=2:X3=0:X4=0:GOSUB 345                    REMARK   ENTER BUYER
        W3S=X0S
        RETURN

5C60    X1=590:X2=6:X3=0:X4=999999:GOSUB 345               REMARK   ENTER CHECK REGISTER NO.
        D(25)=X0
        RETURN

5070    X1=654:GOSUB 673                                   REMARK   ENTER INVOICE DATE
        PRINT
        D(23)=X0
        RETURN

5080    X1=718:GOSUB 673                                   REMARK   ENTER AGE DATE
        PRINT
        D(24)=X0
        RETURN
```

Figure 5.1 *Cont.*

57

Custom Software

The disadvantages to totally prepared (custom) software are the time and expense. The major advantage is that whatever is done should fit what you need for your business. You can have the program written for you by a company or a person that does custom programming for a living (almost every town in the country with a population over 2500 has such an organization*), or you or one of your people can do it. The chances are that once you have gotten some experience with a computer and programming, there will be some routines that you would like created especially for your business. Unless your business is lion farming or xylophone tuning or some other rarity, most everything you can think of in the way of small business applications is already in a prepared state. You may have been sweet-talked into buying a computer that no one has written any canned programs for—then you're stuck. But otherwise, unless you want to spend a lot of time at it, you should not sit down and start to write anything like a payroll system which you can buy for a few hundred dollars and probably have up and running in three weeks. Too many entrepreneurs get an acute case of computer fever, and start playing with the machine to the detriment of their business. Your intent in buying a computer is to improve your business. You don't improve your business by sitting at your computer all day long being enthralled over your newfound skill, finding new ways to calculate *pi* to a million places.

When you choose to have custom software prepared for you, whether by a software house or a private individual, be absolutely certain that whoever does the job understands exactly what you want. Try to be especially clear about what information (input) will be used by the program and what reports (output) you will want. If you goof at the outset and the final product requires modifications, you will pay for it in the end.

Your business may be large enough to justify in-house programming capability. Some entrepreneurs give this responsibility to one of their current employees, whereas others hire someone from the outside. Get some good advice from other business owners or from a computer salesperson before you make a major change such as bringing in a programmer.

Whatever way you choose, be sure that you get what is best for your business at the lowest cost consistent with performance.

Error Messages

You should look carefully at the **error messages** provided by the programs you buy. These messages are notifications by the computer to the operator that he has done something wrong. You want enough of them to prevent you from

* Look in your Yellow Pages under Data Processing Service.

making mistakes that would distort your financial figures. Of course, if you louse up the figures themselves, nothing will help you except detailed attention. The computer will prompt you but it can't eliminate total foolishness. If you do discover a mistake that you made with some past financial information, most programs have methods to go back and fix incorrect data.

Warranties

Some packages have warranties and some are sold "as is." A program with a warranty is guaranteed to work on your equipment. If there are minor problems, you can call either the company that sold you the program or the company that wrote it. They can usually give you a quick solution over the telephone unless the problem is more serious. In that case, you may have to ask for your money back. A program sold "as is" means just what it says. It's like a used car—"you buys the program and you takes your chances." Until you are relatively seasoned in the use of data processing, stay away from "as is" programs, especially if they are critical packages for your business like G/L. You would be pretty safe, on the other hand, with $25 programs for things like balancing your checkbook.

Program Maintenance

The other item to look into is program maintenance. You may have the option of paying a maintenance fee (either one-time or continuing) or it may be built into the purchase price of the software. By paying the fee, you are assured of receiving updates (like new tax withholding schedules in a payroll program) and new coding to fix **bugs** that weren't caught when the program was first released. Bugs in programs are strange animals. When a program is going through its final checks, sample data is run for which the final results are known. If the answers are correct, the program is assumed to be okay. Every seasoned programmer knows, however, that there are bugs in the program that may not show up for a long time, and when they are discovered (usually by some hapless user), they have to be fixed. A brief story (true, by the way) follows, to illustrate.

A friend of the author worked on a payroll program for the Commonwealth of Massachusetts in the mid-1960's. In those days, there was a big push by many employers, especially government agencies, to have employees sign up to buy U.S. Savings Bonds. The normal procedure was for employees to agree to some deduction from their pay to buy the bonds. The deduction was to be an amount that would let them purchase an entire bond after a certain number of deductions. The minimum allowable deduction was $6.25, which was one-third of the $18.75 needed to buy one $25.00 Series E bond. Most state employees would use that particular system, it was thought. The programmer who worked on the payroll program created, as one option, a bond deduction program that would allow an employee to accumulate three months' deductions of $6.25 per month, and at the end of the third month, the computer would issue a $25.00 bond. But after the payroll program had been running for a while, a number of employees who were under the minimum deduction began to complain about getting a $25.00 bond. It was eventually discovered that what they really wanted was to let nine deposits of $6.25 build up until they had enough for a $75.00 bond. Sounds silly, losing the interest? Yes, it is silly, but some facts came out of an investigation:

- Most of the state employees of Massachusetts work in Boston.
- The majority of the people in Boston are Roman Catholics—heavily Irish.
- The $25.00 bond has a picture of George Washington—a WASP.
- The $75.00 bond has a picture of John F. Kennedy—a Massachusetts Irish Roman Catholic.

Anyway, the program was fixed to accommodate those people who wanted to see JFK, not Washington, on their bonds.

Business Programs

Most canned programs today are self-explanatory, and can be up and running on your computer quickly and easily, as long as you buy the right packages for your computer model and configuration and as long as you minimize any changes. The time to get the application fully operational will be determined by your ability to feed your business's data into the proper file or files. As we said earlier, almost any normal business application that you can think of has been written as a computer program; the only restriction will be either computer or media compatibility and even some of that apparent mismatch can be gotten around. The most common small business applications available today are:

- general ledger accounting
- accounts payable
- accounts receivable
- inventory
- payroll

Word processing (WP), the capability of a machine to handle, move, and rearrange text, is also popular. It is not listed with the five areas above however, because it is a separate function, not a true business data processing (DP) operation. There are general accounting packages available which integrate the five business functions into one package. We will have more to say about WP following the discussion of basic business programs. What follows is a general description of what these applications require, how they work, and what they provide.

General Ledger Accounting

Some of what will be said under the general ledger (G/L) description will be true of almost any business application. For instance, any business package that you buy—including the general ledger—should be interactive in nature, in that the program will ask yes/no questions, or will ask you to make a selection, or will ask you to make an entry of some kind.

Most people reading this book, we assume, have some knowledge of accounting theory and practice. We will not turn this chapter into a primer in bookkeeping, but instead present a brief overview of what goes on to help set the stage before we continue.

Figure 5.2 shows the general flow of accounting information within a computerized G/L program. The first step is the creation of some piece of original data as a function of a business transaction of one kind or another. The most common transactions are the receipt of cash or the creation of an account receivable, both from sales and the disbursement of cash, or the creation of an account payable as the result of an expense or purchase. In the establishment of a full audit trial, it is important that the original data portion have some reconciling document—like a sales slip—to back up the transaction. Using a computer, it is not necessary to have handwritten original books of entry (journals and ledgers) although it isn't a bad idea to back the computer up with something in writing. Most G/L programs available have the ability to create journals (the original entries themselves) and ledgers (transactions grouped into convenient headings like "Cash In Bank" or "Wages Paid").

Like an accountant, G/L programs work with debits and credits. As you probably know, debits (abbreviated "dr" for some unknown reason) and credits (abbreviated "cr" for a known reason) are simply additions or subtractions to particular accounts. In double-entry accounting, the debits always equal the credits. The following chart will help you remember how debits and credits are treated:

Item	An Increase Is a	A Decrease Is a
Assets	debit	credit
Liabilities and Equities	credit	debit
Sales	credit	debit
Expenses	debit	credit

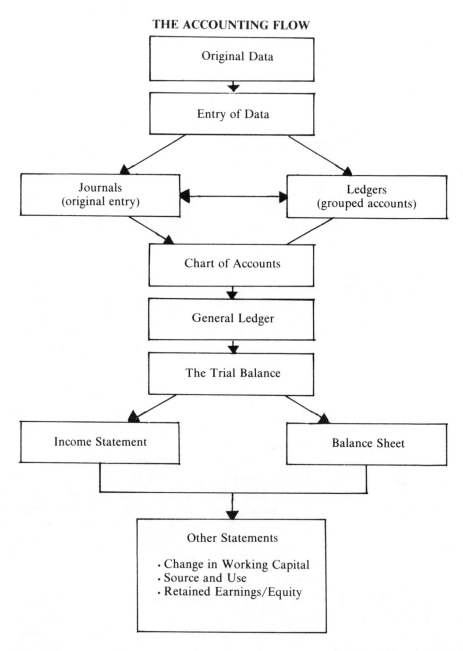

THE ACCOUNTING FLOW

Figure 5.2 *The general flow of accounting information within a computerized G/L program.*

Suppose you operate a small store and someone buys something from you for $1.00 that you paid $.50 for. In receiving that $1.00, you have experienced a sale *and* you have increased your cash on hand at the same time, thus the "double entry". In accounting terminology, the offsetting transactions would look like this:

Notice that the increase in cash (an asset) is a debit (dr) whereas the increase in sales is a credit and they are offsetting and equal.

The process is not over. Your customer removed something from your store, therefore, your inventory (asset) decreased, but cost of goods sold (expense) increased. Another accounting must be made:

	Inventory			*Cost of Goods Sold*	
Dr		Cr	Dr		Cr
		.50	.50		

In doing the trial balance, the report would look like this:

XYZ Company
Trial Balance

	Dr	Cr
Cash	1.00	
Inventory		.50
Sales		1.00
Cost of Goods Sold	.50	
TOTALS	1.50	1.50

and the totals balance.

A computer could do most of this automatically. You would have to tell it:

- what accounts are affected (e.g., cash)
- the amount of the transaction ($1.00)
- whether the transaction is a debit or a credit (debit, in this case)

To get going with most G/L programs, you need to establish a parameter file. Although the information to be given to this file varies, some typical parameters may include:

- name and address of your company
- department names or numbers
- titles of various reports
- format of reports
- an option that shows previous period data (last month, last year)
- whether percentages are to be shown or not

Chart of Accounts. Usually, but not always, the next task is to establish the chart of accounts—a listing of all the accounts (cash, marketable securities, wages payable, utilities) that your business uses or will use. The manual that you receive with your G/L or accounting package will specify both the numbering and naming scheme to be used. The naming is up to you, but you should pick names that are meaningful in accounting terms (you should not label "cash on hand" as "greens in my jeans"). The numbering system should also follow some normal convention, for instance:

- Assets begin with 1, or 10, or 100.
- Liability accounts start with a 2, or 20, or 200.
- Equity accounts start with 3.
- Revenue accounts are a 4.
- Expense items are 5.
- Miscellaneous items are 6.

Further breakdowns are possible, such as the example given below for current assets:

```
10000 ASSETS
  10100 CURRENT ASSETS
    10110 CASH
      10111 currency
      10112 checking accounts
      10113 savings accounts
      10114 certificates of deposit
      10115 miscellaneous
    10120 ACCOUNTS RECEIVABLE
      10121 0–30 days
      10122 31–60 days
      10123 61–90 days
      10124 Over 90 days
    10130 INVENTORY
      10131 raw materials
      10132 work in process
      10133 finished goods
    10140 ACCRUALS
    10150 OTHER CURRENT ASSETS
```

Even more detail would be possible in some cases. The CURRENCY account could be expanded to include sub-categories like petty cash. Departments or profit centers can also be established if the user finds this approach helpful.

Don't get worried if you do not create all the accounts that you might use in the beginning. Most programs have the option to create a new account at any time. This option is part of the program **menu** which displays an array of choices available. For instance, suppose that your G/L program was running for a while and you suddenly found the need to create a new asset account called PREPAID RENT which was a current asset. In bringing up your G/L program, the screen might display the following menu:

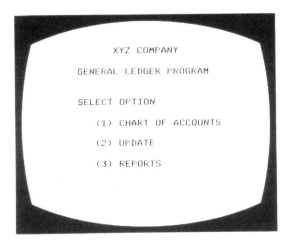

XYZ COMPANY

GENERAL LEDGER PROGRAM

SELECT OPTION

(1) CHART OF ACCOUNTS

(2) UPDATE

(3) REPORTS

If you type in a "1" followed by some other key (usually the RETURN key on the keyboard), the screen might then show a new menu:

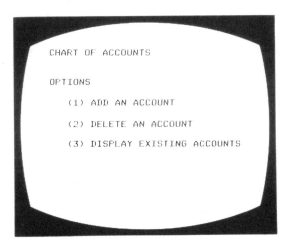

CHART OF ACCOUNTS

OPTIONS

(1) ADD AN ACCOUNT

(2) DELETE AN ACCOUNT

(3) DISPLAY EXISTING ACCOUNTS

If you then enter another "1," the computer would ask you the number and name of the account that you want to add. You might use 10141 PREPAID RENT. Notice that the first four digits (1014) would place the account under the general heading of ACCRUALS. After you have added the new account, go back and ask the computer to display all the existing accounts to be sure that the new account has been received correctly.

Depending upon the particular program, you may be able to start working with your G/L after the chart of accounts has been prepared. Some packages offer different options, usually having to do with report formatting, for you to select. You may be able to choose comparative financial statements, percentage comparisons, financial ratios, or various intermediate reports.

Let's assume that you are ready to begin actual operation. The first task will be to enter various transactions for a certain period. Quite possibly, you will have to "bring the program up to date" by entering past financial information. You want the program to be able to serve pretty much the same function as your accountant, so you will have to supply the necessary historical data. Some programs feature a sample G/L entry with known answers which will give you a chance to get used to how the program works before you hopelessly muddy up your own data.

Many people enter their transactions daily, but you may want to go every other day or even weekly. This group of transactions is known as a "batch"— not to be confused with computer **batch processing**. When you make the entries you will probably have to be careful about the debits-equals-credits business; that is, you will have to learn a little accounting theory. A text in bookkeeping, available at any bookstore for under $5.00, will give you the basics.

Figure 5.3 is a hypothetical example of a summary, or proof, of batch totals for XYZ Company. Note that entries grouped together in the REFERENCE DATA column will balance—the first entry, CASH SALES of $27,000.00, is offset by an increase (debit) in CURRENCY of $27,000. In December, XYZ collected $34,000.00 of receivables due in less than 30 days, $19,000.00 of receivables due in 31–60 days, and $6,000.00 of receivables due in 61–90 days. Since these three receivables categories produced cash which was deposited in the company's checking account, the receivables (credits) were offset by a $59,000.00 increase (debit). After the appropriate entries are made, the program will total the debit and credit columns; the two totals should be equal. If they are not, some programs will help you to pin down the error.

When these transactions are being made, they are not usually entered or posted to the general ledger. The reason for this is that items may have to be added, deleted, or changed. A review of activity, like that shown in Figure 5.3, allows changes to be made before they become a permanent part of the accounting records.

Once the batch proof is verified as being correct, it is posted to the general ledger. It is a good idea to get a hard copy (printed page) of the batch proof for

DATE: 12/31/XX

XYZ COMPANY

GENERAL LEDGER PROGRAM

BATCH TOTALS

ACCOUNT NO.	ACCOUNT NAME	DATE	REFERENCE DATA	AMOUNTS DR	AMOUNTS CR
40010	CASH SALES	12/31/XX	REVENUE JOURNAL, DEC XX		27,000.00
40020	CREDIT SALES	12/31/XX	REVENUE JOURNAL, DEC XX		58,000.00
10111	CURRENCY	12/31/XX	REVENUE JOURNAL, DEC XX	27,000.00	
10121	ACCOUNTS RECEIVABLE	12/31/XX	REVENUE JOURNAL, DEC XX	58,000.00	
10121	ACCOUNTS RECEIVABLE	12/31/XX	RECEIPTS, DEC XX		34,000.00
10122	ACCOUNTS RECEIVABLE	12/31/XX	RECEIPTS, DEC XX		19,000.00
10123	ACCOUNTS RECEIVABLE	12/31/XX	RECEIPTS, DEC XX		6,000.00
10112	CHECKING ACCOUNTS	12/31/XX	RECEIPTS, DEC XX	59,000.00	
50143	TELEPHONE	12/31/XX	DISBURSEMENTS, DEC XX	1,200.00	
50217	ELECTRICITY	12/31/XX	DISBURSEMENTS, DEC XX	400.00	
50320	RENT	12/31/XX	DISBURSEMENTS, DEC XX	1,000.00	
50402	ACCOUNTS PAYABLE	12/31/XX	DISBURSEMENTS, DEC XX	28,000.00	
50510	TAXES	12/31/XX	DISBURSEMENTS, DEC XX	500.00	
10112	CHECKING ACCOUNTS	12/31/XX	DISBURSEMENTS, DEC XX		31,100.00
TOTALS				175,100.00	175,100.00

Figure 5.3 *A hypothetical summary, or proof, of batch totals for XYZ Company.*

XYZ COMPANY
GENERAL LEDGER
DECEMBER 19XX

ACCOUNT NO.	ACCOUNT NAME	DATE	AMOUNTS DR	CR	REFERENCE DATA
40010	CASH SALES	12/1/XX		150,000.00	OPENING BALANCE
		12/31/XX		27,000.00	REV JOURNAL, DEC XX
40020	CREDIT SALES	12/1/XX		214,000.00	OPENING BALANCE
		12/31/XX		58,000.00	REV JOURNAL, DEC XX
10111	CURRENCY	12/1/XX	5,000.00		OPENING BALANCE
		12/31/XX	27,000.00		REV JOURNAL, DEC XX

Figure 5.4 *Typical printout of general ledger detail.*

XYZ COMPANY
TRIAL BALANCE
DECEMBER 19XX

ACCOUNT NO.	ACCOUNT NAME	OPENING BALANCE	AMOUNTS DR	CR	ENDING BALANCE
10111	CURRENCY	150,000.00		27,000.00	177,000.00 CR
40010	CASH SALES	214,000.00		58,000.00	272,000.00 CR
40020	CREDIT SALES	5,000.00	27,000.00		32,000.00 DR

Figure 5.5 *A sample trial balance report.*

future reference, to help provide an audit trial, and as backup in case some computer problem occurs in the future. Figure 5.4 shows a rather typical print-out of general ledger detail produced from data in Figure 5.3. Note that the opening balance for December 1st is shown and then any and all transactions are detailed below it. In the example in Figure 5.4, there is only one monthly transaction shown in each of the three sample accounts demonstrated; in most actual cases, there would be a number of separate transactions.

Trial Balance. Another report that must be provided for you is the trial balance. A brief sample is shown in Figure 5.5. The debits and credits are summarized (subtotaled), and if a full trial balance were shown, the debits would equal the credits.

At the end of an accounting period (a month, a quarter, a year), the books are closed; that is, no more transactions for that period can be entered. With most packages available today, books can be closed with a single command (CLOSE BOOK, for example) and you are then ready for the financial statements to be prepared. The first two and most important of these statements are the income statement and the balance sheet, shown in Figures 5.6 and 5.7 respectively.

Many other options may be available to you with a G/L package, including:

- other "final" reports such as the Source and Use of Funds Statement, Changes in Financial Position, Statement of Retained Earnings
- check and/or daily deposit registers
- percentages that expense items are of net sales on the income statement
- financial ratios (touched on later in this chapter)

Of all the programs available, the G/L package is the most important since its primary task is to prepare key financial statements (income statement and balance sheet) and to hold the basic fiscal records of the business. It is up to you whether you buy a G/L program as a separate system or whether you go for a full accounting program which will tie in with inventory, billing, payables, receivables, payroll—all the subsidiary but necessary procedures that eventually have an effect on the financial matters and statements of the business.

Accounts Payable

As we said earlier, the accounts payable (A/P) program can be a stand-alone program, it can be fully integrated into a full accounting program, or it can be something in-between—a program whose output is later fed into a G/L program. We highly recommend the integrated package. If you do go the separate package route for one reason or another, you should buy the A/P package from the same software house that wrote the G/L. This is another place to ask for help from your hardware salesperson.

```
                        INCOME STATEMENT
                              OF
                         XYZ COMPANY

             for the year ended December 31, 19XX



Net Sales                                                    $100,000

      Cost of Goods Sold
            Inventory Jan. 1       $ 10,000
            Purchases                40,000
            Goods Available        $ 50,000
            Inventory Dec. 31        15,000

                 Cost of Goods Sold                            35,000

         Gross Margin                                        $ 65,000



Expenses

      Rent                         $  6,000
      Wages                          17,000
      Supplies                        2,000
      Advertising                     1,000
      Insurance                       1,000
      Delivery Cost                   2,000
      Depreciation                    1,700
      Taxes Paid                      1,000
      Utilities                       2,000
      Maintenance                     1,000
      Miscellaneous                   3,000

            Total Expenses                                   $ 37,700

         Net Profit                                          $ 27,300
```

Figure 5.6 *A sample income statement.*

An account payable is a future obligation of your business to pay money to some other business, institution, or individual as a result of your having ordered and received acceptable goods or services. Although notes payable (repayment of a form of debt which usually includes interest due) are handled differently in an accounting sense, most A/P packages treat the current portions of debt in much the same way as a trade account payable.

Accounts payable management is, like so many other "systems" of your business, vital to the continued success of your enterprise. Most suppliers are will-

```
                    BALANCE SHEET
                          OF
                     XYZ COMPANY

                as of December 31, 19XX

CURRENT ASSETS                  CURRENT LIABILITIES

   Cash                $ 3,000     Accounts Payable      $ 1,500
   Accounts Receivable   5,700     Notes Payable           1,000
   Inventory             6,800     Other Accruals          2,000

   Total Current Assets $15,500    Total Current
                                   Liabilities           $ 4,500


FIXED ASSETS                    FIXED LIABILITIES

   Equipment and                   Long Term Debt        $ 5,000
   Fixtures            $18,200
     Depreciation       (1,000)    Total Liabilities     $ 9,500
   Truck                 4,900
     Depreciation       (1,500)    Net Worth
   Total Fixed Assets  $20,600     Proprietorship        $26,600




Total Assets          $36,100   Liabilities & Net Worth  $36,100
```

Figure 5.7 *A sample balance sheet.*

ing to supply goods and services to you on their normal credit terms, that is, they expect you to pay for these goods and services after a normal lapse of time as long as you got what you ordered and it was in the condition that the supplier advertised or purported it to be. Payables management means cash management. Many small-business owners have no real schedule for paying their bills. Some owners do it on one particular day of the week, some pay right away even though the supplier does not require it, some wait until the supplier starts screaming. Basically, you want to stretch your payables out to the time limit consistent with good business practice. The longer that cash remains in your accounts, the longer you can use it, but if you wait too long on payables, you will damage your credit standing and that may even bring you to the point where shipments to you may be stopped.

Figure 5.8 shows a typical accounts payable cycle. The process begins when an order is placed with a supplier. The goods (services) are delivered along with an invoice (bill). If the goods or services are acceptable, an account payable is

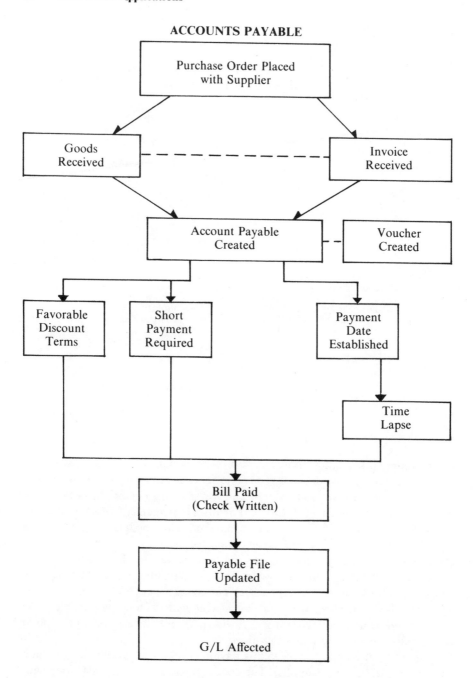

Figure 5.8 *A typical accounts payable (A/P) cycle.*

created to reflect the amount due the supplier. As a part of good accounting practice, a voucher—a physical document that directs the payment of an obligation—is also created; its creation presupposes that the check to be written for payment has been approved by someone in control. Vouchers can also be set up on a prepaid basis (like a pro forma or COD payment) and merely become matters of record.

One of the first steps in getting started with an A/P software package is to establish two separate files: a list of accounts to which payables will be assigned and a list of vendors (suppliers). Figure 5.9 shows some typical accounts to which payables could be assigned. The account numbers and names should be

Figure 5.9 *Typical accounts to which payables could be assigned.*

XYZ COMPANY

ACCOUNTS PAYABLE LIST

ACCOUNT NO.	ACCOUNT NAME
10131	RAW MATERIALS (INVENTORY)
10210	FIXED ASSETS
50110	INDIRECT MATERIALS
50120	SUPPLIES, OFFICE
50130	SUPPLIES, OTHER
50140	WAGES
50150	SALARIES
50160	TAX, FEDERAL WITHHOLDING
50170	FICA
50180	TAX, STATE WITHHOLDING
50210	ADVERTISING
50220	TELEPHONE
50230	FUEL OIL
50240	ELECTRICITY
50250	RENT
50260	REPAIRS, BUILDING
50270	REPAIRS, EQUIPMENT
50280	REPAIRS, AUTOMOBILE
50310	INSURANCE

identical to those used in the G/L program. Figure 5.10 is a sample vendor list. In addition to the basic information of address and phone, there may be sufficient fields to put in varying code data such as the normal terms of the supplier, whether a discount is available for prompt payment, and special designations for "vendors" like a bank or the IRS. Such a list can be sorted alphabetically by name, numerically by Zip code, or any other way that makes sense. The file could be used to produce mailing labels as well. This particular example shows a six-digit vendor code; some programs may allow more or less than six. If you do not presently use a vendor code, going to a new A/P program may give you the opportunity to create a coding scheme that will help to identify vendors in one way or another.

The largest single benefit of an A/P program is better cash management. A good package enables you to forecast cash requirements based on when accounts are scheduled to be paid, in terms of discounts that may be available, due dates, or overdue conditions. Invoices can be vouchered as they are received for close accounting control. Most programs will automatically calculate the amount of discounts available. Some programs allow the user to assign a particular status to the vouchers such as:

- pay on a normal basis on the date specified at the amount specified
- pay on a date specified and take the discount allowed
- pay a partial amount
- hold payment
- prepaid voucher
- credit memo

Although each commercially available package has a slightly different format, payables are usually entered into the program in a straightforward manner. Some of the better programs present a facsimile image of a voucher form to prompt the operator to enter all the data that will be required for full and proper processing.

Various programs produce various kinds of intermediate reports for the user before the final stages of check writing or posting to the G/L are accomplished. Some of these reports are merely intermediate checks or proofs in the payables process, whereas others are more for the small-business owner's analysis and cash planning.

One such intermediate report should be a straight listing of all the accounts payable by account (not vendor) and should show:

- account number and name
- vendor number and name
- voucher number(s)
- invoice number(s) and date(s)
- amount due on each invoice
- total amount due for that account

XYZ COMPANY

ACCOUNTS PAYABLE

VENDORS

ACCOUNT NO.	NAME	ADDRESS	TELEPHONE	CODES 1	2	3	4
104017	AAA INDUSTRIAL SUPPLY	256 MAIN STREET BOSTON, MA 02162	617-527-7248				
716214	ABLE MACHINE TOOL CO. ATTN: HARRIET JONES	42 APPIAN WAY KEENE, NH 03431	603-357-0123				
015727	ACME CLEANING CO. ATTN: ACCOUNTS REC.	444 MADISON AVE RUTLAND, VT 05401	802-251-1146				
204217	BERKELEY GARAGE ATTN: JOHN BERKELEY	14 ELLIOT STREET BRATTLEBORO, VT 05301	802-254-0515				
992147	BURLINGTON SAVINGS BANK COMMERCIAL LOAN DEPT	ONE ALLEN PLACE BURLINGTON, VT 05517	802-767-1000				

Figure 5.10 *A sample vendor list.*

Naturally, other reports could be prepared. One report which is vital to cash planning is the aged accounts payable which shows some of the above information but may present the data in a time sequence when payments are due. An aged payables report may be done strictly by the date that payments are due, or it may be by vendor, which would also show overdue invoices grouped into amounts due in the next 30 days from the date that the report is requested from the computer; and amounts due in 31–60, 61–90, and over 90 categories.

The A/P package can write the checks and the check stubs, specifying invoice number(s) and date(s) and voucher number(s), and then produce a check register which summarizes all the checks written on a particular day or within a particular period.

Other features to look for in an A/P program are:

- ability to handle multiple checking accounts
- ease of making payments out of the ordinary routine of invoice-voucher-check-register
- security features which prevent unauthorized entry into the program
- automatic generation of recurring payables like a loan repayment
- error checking (idiot-proof) subroutines

Accounts Receivable

One of the vital segments of your business is credit and collection. There is always a question in the mind of small business owners as to whether they should extend credit or not. Most small retail establishments and hospitality businesses do not allow their customers to use any credit other than major credit cards like VISA, MasterCard, or American Express. If your business is service-connected, distributive, or manufacturing, however, you probably will use credit sales. The theory behind using trade credit is that you will increase sales. The problem with credit, as you are well aware, is that you may get into a position where the bulk of your potential cash flow is tied up in doubtful accounts receivable as a result of your granting credit to unworthy customers, or your inability to collect receivables, or both. Your capital has already been used in the creation of a finished product—the investment on your part has been made and you have not been paid. The longer that you wait for payment, the longer you go without cash and the more you lose on the sale.

The job of any good accounts receivable (A/R) program is to take the detailed work of A/R creation, aging, billing, and dunning away from you or your accountant. In the first instance, it gives you more time for being creative in your business and in the second it saves you money.

Figure 5.11 is a graphic representation of an accounts receivable cycle. Much of the report generation can be accomplished with a computer. A good A/R package should provide:

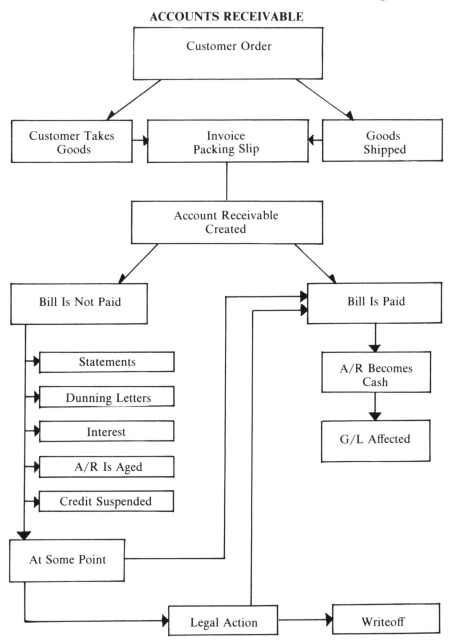

Figure 5.11 *A typical accounts receivable (A/R) cycle.*

- journal transactions for a G/L package
- reporting of credit limits for customers
- calculation of late charges and interest penalties
- a clear audit trail from the entry of the original data through to final reports and G/L
- aging of A/R
- dunning letters (reminder notices)
- reports on customers who may have exceeded their credit limit, past due invoices, overpaid and underpaid invoices, outstanding invoices, late charges, and transactions in general

An order for a good or service from one of your company's credit-approved customers creates a backlog or an unfilled order. All credit customers should be maintained on a customer master file. The format of this file will vary from program to program, but might look something like Figure 5.12. The "credit rating" column generally uses one of the standard rating schemes, such as those issued by Dun & Bradstreet. The "credit limit" column is self-explanatory.

When the customer's order is filled and shipped, the computer prepares a multiform document which serves as an invoice to be mailed to the customer, a packing list which accompanies the goods (but blocks out the price information), and internal copies for control.

All A/R packages produce invoices, although the format will vary from program to program. Unless your business has some unique requirements, you should try to adapt your information to the invoice format provided by the program. Some customers have requirements that must be followed if you are to be paid promptly. Your customer may ask for invoices in triplicate, for example or, as is the case with very large, multiple-location firms, the ordering, shipping, and billing addresses may all be different and you will be required to show all three on the invoice to assure rapid payment. At a minimum, the invoice should show

- customer's purchase order number and date
- your invoice number and date
- date of shipment
- customer's and your part number
- item description
- quantity shipped; portion not shipped (back ordered)
- unit price
- extended price (quantity times unit price)
- customer number
- date invoice is due and appropriate terms of the invoice
- total amount of the invoice

As your business continues to provide goods and services on credit, a file of accounts receivable will be created. You will want the option of "aging" the

XYZ COMPANY

ACCOUNTS RECEIVABLE

CUSTOMER MASTER LIST

CUSTOMER NO.	NAME	ADDRESS	TELEPHONE	RATING	CREDIT LIMIT
106147	BEAUDRY, WALTER CONTRACTOR	414 ELM ST. PROVIDENCE, RI 05172	401-155-6712	Aab	25,000
742530	LAVALLEY SUPPLY	20 HIGH ST. HARTFORD, CT 06801	203-572-7211	bbb	2,000
612341	CONTINENTAL CORP.	CHARLESTOWN RD. BRIDGEPORT,CT 06840	203-672-1417	bbb	3,000
887213	POST ENGINEERING	150 PINE ST. HOOKSET, NH 03150	603-722-9900	aaa	5,000

Figure 5.12 *A typical customer master file for credit customers.*

receivables at any time. With an aging report you can do any number of things like putting a customer on credit hold (no more credit sales until all or a portion of their overdue account is paid) or writing off an uncollectable receivable, or sending nasty letters. A simplified sample of an aging report is shown in Figure 5.13.

It is also possible to use the aging report for analysis because a collection schedule will have been established based on company history. Suppose, for example, that the owner of XYZ Company knows that 80 percent of all receivables in the 31–60 day category are usually collected within the coming 30 days. Using the information provided by a report such as the one in Figure 5.13, the owner could project that $560 (80 percent of the $700 that is the 31–60 day figure) would be received during the coming 30 days. Another analysis that could be done is the percentage breakdown of receivables. For instance, XYZ has $375, or 15 percent, of its receivables in the "over 90" category. As receivables get older they stand a lesser chance of being collected and procedures

Figure 5.13 *A sample aging report for accounts receivable.*

XYZ COMPANY

AGED ACCOUNTS RECEIVABLE

October 1, 19XX

DAYS PAST DUE

NAME	BALANCE	0 – 30	31 – 60	61 – 90	over 90
M. Jones	$ 375	$ 75	$ 300	$ –	$ –
H. Harris	160	60	50	50	–
G. Salzman	50	50	–	–	–
P. Miller	500	300	100	100	–
G. Geipel	50	–	–	50	–
B. Thompson	75	–	75	–	–
H. Strauss	135	100	–	35	–
J. Hegner	125	–	–	–	125
T. Nathan	400	–	100	100	200
A. Cohen	425	400	25	–	–
G. Young	75	25	50	–	–
J. Osborn	200	100	–	50	50
Totals	$2,570	$1,110	$ 700	$ 385	$ 375
%	100	43	27	15	15

stronger than normal billing may have to be used—giving the acount over to an attorney or a collection agency, or both.

Most A/R programs have the ability to generate dunning (reminder) letters. Some users have the computer generate a letter every 30 days along with a statement of overdue account and late charges. The first letter (60 days or so after the invoice date) is nice and chatty—"Didn't you forget something?" The fourth or fifth one threatens to break the customer's legs, sell his or her children into slavery, and send the entire account off for collection. Use automatic letters with extreme care. One large company in the Northeast almost lost its two largest and most profitable customers because of a computer and an over-zealous but lazy credit manager.

Most A/R packages can provide sales reports in various ways. You may wish to see sales information by region of the country; customer Standard Industrial Classification (SIC)—that is, type of customer; time period (month, quarter, year-to-date); previous periods (last month, last year); number of invoices; or average amount per invoice.

Other analyses may also be provided: number of overdue accounts by time period; amount of bad debt allowances; and late charges.

One report that will be of benefit to you is a straight listing of all invoices used either in a particular period or within a certain numerical sequence. This report, normally called an invoice proof, shows invoice number and date; customer name and number; part number and/or part description; and total amount of the invoice. A hypothetical example is shown in Figure 5.14.

When full or partial payment of an invoice is received, the computer program should be able to handle this easily. The program should not do illogical things like automatically apply a partial payment to the newest invoice. Changes to the data files, such as the addition of a new customer, should also be done without complication.

Inventory Control

Finding a computerized inventory control package that fits your particular business may require a little more work than locating a general ledger program. The problem is to find the routine that most closely resembles the way you do business. Wholesale or retail establishments have most of their investment in the finished goods of others—this investment may represent the majority of the business's assets outside of the real estate. Hospitality operations (hotels, inns, restaurants) have a unique inventory situation; service firms may have no inventory at all. Compared to retail and wholesale businesses, a manufacturing concern has three distinct and separate categories of inventory:

> *Raw materials:* items and substances purchased for future conversion which are to be placed into the production operation but which have not been changed from their original state, thus, they have not absorbed any expenses. Economists might say that they have no manufacturing value added to them.

XYZ COMPANY

ACCOUNTS RECEIVABLE

INVOICE LIST

INVOICE NUMBER	DATE	NUMBER	CUSTOMER NAME	ITEM DESCRIPTION	AMOUNT
B0141	5/20/XX	714612	ABC SUPPLY	NAPKINS	$ 313.42
B0142	5/20/XX	04319	HEREFORD	CURTAINS	1,421.08
B0143	5/20/XX	553427	SPOFFORD MFG.	SILVERWARE	3,750.00
B0144	5/21/XX	705064	PROSPECT	WINDOW DRAPES	927.63
B0145	5/21/XX	221027	KENDALL	MISCELLANEOUS	1,985.44
B0146	5/24/XX	903106	AMES CO.	BEDSPREADS	2,417.00
B0147	5/24/XX	462175	AMES CO.	PILLOW CASES	512.60
				TOTAL:	$11,327.17

Figure 5.14 *A hypothetical invoice proof.*

Work in process: the sum total of all parts, subassemblies, and materials that are somewhere in conversion.
Finished goods: items which are complete and ready to ship to customers.

If you have purchased a total accounting package which includes an inventory control program, then you may be able to make use of it or not. If you have to go looking for one, be certain that you understand the nature of your own inventory system.

Some inventory programs come with a purchasing segment. Experts disagree on whether such a purchasing package really belongs with an inventory program, or should be more closely linked with an accounts payable program. Since more and more businesses are becoming totally integrated systems, the argument is rather academic. We favor a purchasing system tied in with the inventory package, and therefore will include it in this section. A good purchasing system (not necessarily an automated one) allows for supplier selection and for the review of supplier performance, both based on price, delivery, quality, service, terms, past reputation.

Years ago, purchasing meant buying—that was all there was to it. Unfortunately, many small businesses today still "buy" and rarely "purchase." Some owners look for the quickest way out of a supply problem by going to a vendor who happens to be convenient. There are dangers that may result from not choosing suppliers carefully, or not using a reasonably formal system of purchasing:

- The price you pay may not be the lowest consistent with the quality that you require.
- The supplier may not be reputable.
- You may deny yourself tax credits or deductions due to incomplete paperwork.
- Good audit trials may not be established.

Business owners who use accountants sparingly may wonder why their operations need good audit trails since they have no outside partners or stockholders. The first reason is the IRS who may audit the tax returns of the business. The second, and more important, reason is the fact that your business will change hands someday (you will sell it or bequeath it) and the lack of well-established procedures and substantiation of process may harm the business's transfer.

One of the primary jobs of a computer purchasing package is the issuance of purchase orders. The P.O. begins the entire process in the purchasing cycle. It can be issued for a one-time purchase (a new delivery truck) or for recurring purchases (inventory). In the latter case, the P.O. is called a blanket order and covers a minimum quantity of goods or services over a fixed time period, usually one year. While P.O. forms vary from one business to another, some of the information that you will want on the document includes:

- P.O. number and date
- vendor number, name, and address
- expected terms and delivery
- reference to a previous telephone order, a previously negotiated blanket order, or a formal price quotation
- vendor's part number and item description, quantity ordered, unit price, extended price
- reference to your internal account number to which the item will be assigned (office supplies, raw material inventory, repairs and maintenance)

The P.O. is issued to the vendor and copies are retained in the business for future reference. When the goods or services ordered are received or completed, the P.O. can be used as a control document to assure that what was ordered was received. That alone is justification to use a formal P.O. system rather than verbal orders. Usually, one of the copies of the P.O. that is sent to the vendor is an acknowledgment copy that the vendor signs and returns to you. This lets you know that the supplier received the order and agrees to its terms. In essence, the acknowledgment completes the contractual cycle.

When the goods (or services) are delivered, along with the supplier's invoice, they can be matched against the P.O. If everything is in order, an account payable can be created for that program to handle.

One very helpful feature of a purchasing package is the provision of automatic reminders of overdue shipments. For example, you might want to receive a report on, say, Friday for items that are overdue that day and possibly items that are due to be received the coming week. Another useful feature is vendor analysis—how many times a supplier has been late on promised delivery (and by how many days each time), and which suppliers shipped or supplied items that had to be returned for one reason or another.

There are several categories of "purchases."

- "required" purchases—licenses and taxes
- "involuntary" purchases—electric power and telephone
- services—plumbing and roof repair
- assets required in the business—office equipment, machines, cash registers, vehicles
- inventory items

The remainder of this section will be addressed to this final category.

Inventory control means a lot more than just knowing how many of something is on hand. The purchase of a good inventory control program may be one of the best investments that you have ever made for your business, especially if you buy for resale. It is not uncommon for medium-sized retail stores to have 25,000 different items in their inventory.

Regarding inventory for resale, there are two measurements which are critical to the success of your business. The first is return on your investment which directly reflects the markup on your cost. This is known as gross margin. The second is inventory turnover—theoretically, the number of times that an inventory level is replenished and then sold.

Good inventory packages deal primarily with these qualities and their many ramifications. Thus, we will treat each area separately even though they are closely related.

In terms of return on investment, the inventory program should provide information on the cost of goods sold and the value of items left in inventory at any time—in other words, the financial part of the perpetual inventory system. When an item is removed from stock and sold, two accounting activities occur: (1) a sale is made with a certain cost associated with that sale, and (2) the value of inventory (a current asset) is reduced. Any sale that takes place affects the accounting records and it should be the task of the inventory program to make the appropriate adjustments. The value of the cost of goods sold will depend upon the method of valuing inventory that you are using—average cost, last-in-first-out (LIFO), first-in-first-out (FIFO). We are not going to go into a discussion of valuation methods in this book, but any good package will have these options built into it. One report that should be made available to you on a periodic basis is the gross margin on each product classification. This may be provided by the G/L program rather than the inventory control program. The level of gross margin in terms of percentage of sales dollar over time is vitally important to your final net profit figure and can help you determine pricing levels.

The inventory turnover part of the package is most important. As a small business owner with a major investment in inventory, you should have a good handle on:

- What is in your inventory at any given point—type of items, how many, how much they are worth, who supplied them.
- How many items have been added or deleted in the past month, quarter or year.
- What items you will delete from future inventory as a function of low turnover, low margin, or both.
- The minimum (safety stock) and maximum quantities of each and every inventory item that should be on hand at any time.
- The right quantity to order. This is often referred to as the "economic order quantity" and most inventory control programs have this calculation built in.
- The quantity of an item on back order.

When you decide to convert to an inventory control package, you will have to take inventory—a physical count of what you have on hand. Even if you use a manual perpetual inventory (as opposed to a rotating inventory), under no circumstances should you use the recorded count because there might be some rather significant errors in doing that. Take the time to do the physical counting. You might want to install your package at the time that the inventory is to be done, when your inventory should be at its lowest level. If you are planning the conversion to coincide with a normal inventory count, be sure that you have read over the documentation that is supplied so that you are aware of such things as how many characters are allowed to describe a particular item. Then you can do the count and prepare data for computer entry at the same time. Figure 5.15 is a sample of a worksheet used to take a physical inventory. You could make up blank sheets like this, keeping in mind the following columns that are on the sheet:

XYZ STOCK NO. You may use your own stock numbers which already have meaning to you. There is a good chance that a program will not accept your present numbering scheme and, thus, you will have to change it. This is not a problem, but an opportunity to design a scheme of nomenclature that has some meaning (for example, the lead character can designate a department or a product classification).

SUPPLIER NO. Pay attention to the size and type of field that the program requires, and be sure that the supplier code used here is the same as you have used in the A/P package.

ITEM DESCRIPTION. Use any description which is meaningful but be very careful of any duplication.

COUNT. The physical quantity on hand.

MIN. The safety level below which you do not want stock to fall. (Note: it could be zero.)

MAX. The most that you ever want in stock.

COMMENTS. Self-explanatory.

```
                            XYZ COMPANY
                    PHYSICAL INVENTORY AS OF    _____


ITEM   XYZ STOCK NO.   SUPPLIER NO.   ITEM DESCRIPTION   COUNT    MIN    MAX    COMMENTS

1.

2.

3.

4.

5.

6.

7.

8.
```

Figure 5.15 *A sample worksheet for physical inventory.*

The MIN and MAX quantities already may have been established from past experience or the program may establish them in the future.

One feature of a purchasing/inventory package should be the reorder point. When some quantity is reached in the perpetual inventory, the program could either signal that a reorder point has been established or (in some cases) it could actually issue the P.O.

Once the program is operating it is a simple matter to make changes such as withdrawals from inventory (usually sales) and additions to inventory (normally purchases).

Most inventory packages are menu driven. Your CRT screen might typically show what is in Figure 5.16.

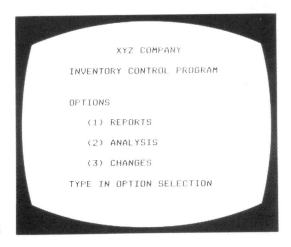

Figure 5.16

Typing in "3" might give a result as in Figure 5.17.

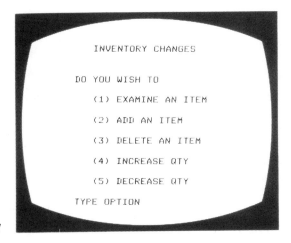

Figure 5.17

If you selected option 4, the computer might ask you to type in the stock number of the item which you wish to increase.

Option 1 in Figure 5.17 allows the user to examine the status of one particular item. This may be required from time to time as a result of a customer's inquiry. If a customer then orders the item, option 5 would be selected to reflect the decrease in quantity as a result of the sale.

The status of the inventory can be provided automatically at the end of any period or on demand by selecting option 1 in Figure 5.16. A typical inventory status report might resemble Figure 5.18. The report is self-explanatory to a large degree; OH stands for the number of units on hand and BO is the number back ordered. The LAST MO. and LAST YR. quantities are provided for planning and ordering purposes.

```
                         XYZ COMPANY

                       INVENTORY STATUS

                                        DATE:    03/07/XX

STOCK NO.         VENDOR NO.        COST    OH    MIN    LAST MO.
NOMENCLATURE      VENDOR NAME       UNIT    BO    MAX    LAST YR.

110742            72347             4.39    24     5        6
BLUE PAINT        ABC SUPPLY         GAL     0    40      129


007241            72347             0.79     0    10       37
SCREWDRIVER       ABC SUPPLY          EA   100   200      342


034170            91993             8.00    12     5        3
PADS, YELLOW      TOWN STATIONERY    DOZ     0    20       57
```

Figure 5.18 *A typical inventory status report.*

Payroll

As a computerized function, payroll has probably been around the longest of any business program. Even though it is the oldest program, it is the one that seems to give most people fits. The reason for this is the thousands of variations that exist from one organization to another, one town to another, one state to another. A few years ago, most small business owners would have been well advised to make out paychecks and the required reports by hand or, at best, to let their bank do it for a few cents per check per week. With the arrival of full accounting programs for small computers, entrepreneurs are well advised to seek out a payroll system that will fit in with the G/L. In this manner, the effects that wage and salary disbursements have on the financial statements can be handled automatically.

We will not go into great detail about payroll since there are so many systems on the market. Just be sure that the program you choose will work easily for your business (especially if you compensate your people in a slightly different way than the majority of other operations*, or if you have unique kinds of deductions). To give you some idea of how a typical payroll system works, we adapted the following general description from a program prepared by Barbara Rush, president of Micro Applications Associates in Mesquite, Texas. The writeup is rather general in its nature, but does refer to some actual procedures that are required and shows some actual commands, to give a rough idea of how programs are addressed and controlled.

The payroll system described here will accept data for employee master records and for the wages to be paid; will produce payroll checks, a labor distribution report, and a payroll journal; can print a copy of the employee master file, employee earnings records, quarterly state tax reports and annual W-2 reports; and will post all accounting entries to the general ledger data files. The tasks in the program itself are listed below.

Enter or Change Employee Master Data. As a first step in the program, you will be asked for an employee number. The system checks this number against the master file, and if it finds the number already exists, you will be asked whether you want to change it. If you answer yes, the information on file for that employee will be displayed; if you answer no, you will be asked for another employee number.

If you are changing data already on the master file, simply type "Return" for any field which you do not want to change. Type "@" to go back to change a field which you hve completed, or use the backspace to change a character in the field being entered. As you complete each form on the screen, you will be asked whether it is okay to continue. If you answer yes, another form of information will be displayed; if you answer no, the cursor (a small line that appears on the screen, used as a guide to tell you where you are) will move back to the first field on the screen so that you may make changes. New data works the same way except that the forms displayed will not show any data in the fields. When you are through making entries to the master file, type "@" in the employee number field. The system will sort and rewrite the employee master file. This may take several minutes, depending on the size of the file.

Enter Balances Forward for Labor Distribution. This routine accepts data for the labor distribution report. The data entered does *not* post the general ledger files.

---

* We heard of one business that buys new cars for employees after a certain number of years of service.

You will first be asked to replace the payroll data disk with the general ledger disk so that the system can read in the chart of accounts. After you have replaced the payroll data disk, the screen will display a form for the labor distribution balances forward. You may type "Return" to skip a field or "@" to go back to change a field.

As you make the entries, a proof sheet will be produced on the printer so that you can check them when complete. When you have finished with the balance forward entries, type "@" in the ledger field and the system will sort and rewrite the labor distribution files. Again, this may take several minutes.

Enter Current Hours and Salary Data. This routine allows you to enter hours for hourly employees and gross pay for salaried employees who are to receive checks. You may make several entries for each employee in order to charge labor to the proper ledgers and cost codes.

You will first be asked to replace the payroll data disk with the general ledger data disk so that the charge of accounts may be read. After you have replaced the payroll data disk, you will be asked for a period ending date. It should be the date through which employees are being paid. In producing the checks, this date will be used to determine which data from the gross pay file is to be used.

You will be asked for the employee number. The system will check the master file and display employee name, salary code, hourly rate or salary, expense ledger, reference, and workman's compensation code for that employee. You may change any of this information (except the name) for this check run only. You may enter regular hours and overtime hours for hourly employees. When you have completed all entries, type "@." The system will sort the data entered by employee number, print a proof list, and return.

Print Checks, Labor Distribution, and Journal. You should have the check forms in the printer when you select this task. If you do not have them lined up correctly, type the "ESC" key to stop the program. You may then realign the checks, type "PR," and the checks will start over.

You will be asked whether you have made a backup disk and posted to the general ledger. These tasks must be completed prior to processing checks. If you answer no, the system will stop this program and return to the main menu.

The system can make two types of deductions from payroll checks. These are only made for those employees who have deduction information on file in their master records. You will be asked whether each type is to be made on this payroll run.

The system will then proceed to print a check for each employee for whom you have entered gross pay data. When it is through, it will sort the labor distribution file and then stop for you to change paper in the printer. The labor distribution report will then be produced. When it is complete, the system does some sorting and rewriting of files and pauses for you to change paper again if you wish to do so. If not, type "Return" and it will continue.

The payroll journal will then be printed and the main menu will be displayed.

Post to General Ledger. As the payroll is being calculated, entries are created which will be posted to the general ledger. When you are ready to transfer this data to the general ledger disk, select this task.

The program will stop and ask that you replace the payroll program disk (not the data disk) with the general ledger data disk. When you have done so, it will read the entries created by the payroll from the payroll data disk and write them on the general ledger data disk. When it is finished, it will ask you to replace the general ledger disk with the payroll program disk.

Print Employee Master File. This program prints the data in the employee master file for your convenience in checking. When it is complete, the main menu is again displayed.

Print Employee Earnings Records. This prints the data from the master file showing gross pay and deductions for each employee. After completion, the main menu is displayed.

End of Period Data Transfer. The payroll master file keeps gross pay data on each employee in three categories: current month, current quarter, and prior quarters. You will be asked whether you want an end of month, end of quarter, or end of year transfer. They should be done in order. Be sure to make a backup disk before running a transfer. Be certain that you have completed all reports for the calendar year before running the end of year transfer as it zeros the earnings for each employee.

This routine can also eliminate terminated employees from the master file if you wish.

No report is produced; the main menu is displayed when the program is complete.

Enter Tax Rates and Ledger Numbers. This routine allows you to change rates for state and federal unemployment and FICA taxes and the ledgers to which these are charged.

When it is complete, the main menu will be displayed.

Print 941 Reports (Quarterly wage and tax statement for the IRS). You will be asked whether you have completed the last payroll for the quarter and made a backup disk. You will also be asked for the report date. You should run 941 reports after the last payroll in a quarter and before the first in the next quarter.

When the report is complete, the main menu is displayed.

Print W-2 Reports. W-2 reports should be printed after the 941's for the last quarter of the year. Like 941 reports, this is a memo run, and the data can be corrected if necessary before reprinting the report.

When the report is complete, the main menu is displayed.

Finished—Exit Payroll Program. This particular payroll system is simple to operate and very straightforward in procedure. The actual operating instructions would have much more detail and would include an explanation of error instructions and "prompts" that the program contains.

Other Business-Connected Programs

We have covered the five major business systems that are readily available for almost every small business and every small computer. Unless your business situation is unique, we highly recommend that you start with these before you try others. As we said before, there are many other application packages available and you can write any programs that you want. Your local computer dealer can give you several catalogs of other packages that you can buy. Before we talk about word processing (WP), we will briefly mention some other applications software that you may want to consider. Some of these applications may be included as part of a much larger package such as general accounting.

Budgetary Control/Forecasting. A good budget program has two separate segments: planning and reporting. The planning portion will allow you to prepare a projected budget like that shown in Figure 5.19. You should then have the ability to change various items and determine the effect on cash flow in future periods. Some programs have an "automatic" feature that allows you to take an item like wages and increase them by a fixed percentage for a designated time period. (In Figure 5.19 we show a six-month projection.) A budget package should allow several years of forward planning as well as both cash and accounting figures; a superimposition of revenue projections for profit planning; the ability to instantaneously change items like loan amounts/ interest rates, methods of depreciation, tax credits to see their effect on the financial data.

Another feature that might be useful is the preparation of pro forma (future) income statements and balance sheets from basic projected assumptions. Another option will be calculations on the amount of future outside (external) funds based upon growth projections. The reporting phase of the budget program will supply information like that in Figure 5.20 to the business owner.

Financial Ratio Analysis. The analysis of financial statements through the use of percentages and ratios is becoming of great importance to small business.

XYZ COMPANY

SIX-MONTH BUDGET

Item						
Wages & Benefits	$ 6,000	$ 6,000	$ 6,500	$ 6,500	$ 6,500	$ 7,000
Travel & Entertainment	100	100	100	100	100	100
Gas & Oil	200	200	200	200	200	200
Repairs & Maintenance	150	-	-	250	-	-
Inventory Purchases	5,000	8,000	6,000	8,000	4,000	2,000
Legal & Accounting	200	200	400	200	200	300
Rent	900	900	900	900	900	900
Loan Repayment	1,100	1,100	1,100	1,100	1,100	1,100
Trash Removal & Snow Plowing	400	300	300	200	200	200
Advertising	1,000	1,000	1,500	1,500	1,500	1,000
Telephone	400	400	400	400	400	500
Electricity	300	300	200	200	100	100
Janitorial Service	200	200	200	200	200	200
Supplies	200	200	200	200	200	200
Taxes & Licenses	100	100	-	-	100	-
Equipment Purchases	200	-	-	1,000	-	2,000
Miscellaneous	200	200	200	200	200	200
TOTAL EXPENSES	$16,650	$19,400	$18,200	$21,150	$15,900	$16,000

Figure 5.19 *A hypothetical six-month budget projection.*

XYZ COMPANY
MONTHLY BUDGET REPORT

	FOR MONTH 3			YEAR-TO-DATE			
ITEM	BUDGET	ACTUAL	Variance (Over) UNDER	BUDGET	ACTUAL	Variance (Over) UNDER	25% of Year Past % Annual Spent
Wages & Benefits	$ 6,500	$ 6,942	$(442)	$18,500	$20,107	$(1,607)	30
Travel & Entertainment	100	212	(112)	300	403	(103)	28
Gas & Oil	200	127	73	600	178	422	18
Repairs & Maintenance	-	516	(516)	150	516	(366)	12
Inventory Purchases	6,000	4,100	1,900	19,000	16,897	2,103	32
Legal & Accounting	400	400	-0-	800	600	200	23
Rent	900	900	-0-	2,700	2,700	-0-	25
Loan Repayment	1,100	1,100	-0-	3,300	3,300	-0-	25
Trash Removal & Snow Plowing	300	243	57	1,000	651	349	20
Advertising	1,500	2,127	(627)	3,500	4,221	(721)	27
Telephone	400	942	(542)	1,200	1,837	(637)	29
Electricity	200	317	(117)	800	714	86	23
Janitorial Service	200	261	(61)	600	552	48	22
Supplies	200	17	183	600	397	203	21
Taxes & Licenses	-	100	(100)	200	100	100	12
Equipment Purchases	-	550	(550)	200	550	(350)	38
Miscellaneous	200	351	(151)	600	607	(7)	24
	$18,200	$19,205	$(1005)	$54,250	$54,330	$(80)	26

Figure 5.20 *A sample budget report.*

Figure 5.21 is a sample of fifteen ratios that might be used. The "Industry" column contains information that would be stored in the program. The values for your business (restaurant, apparel shop) can be obtained from a source such as Robert Morris Associates in Philadelphia.*

RATIO ANALYSIS

XYZ COMPANY

YEAR 19XX

Ratio or Quantity	How Calculated	XYZ	Industry
1. Current Ratio	Current Assets / Current Liabilities		2.1
2. Quick Ratio	C.A. - Inventories / Current Liabilities		0.8
3. Current Liabilities to Tangible Net Worth			61%
4. Net Sales to Tangible Net Worth			5.1
5. Net Sales to W.C.	Net Sales / C.A. - C.L.		12.3
6. Asset Turnover	Net Sales / Total Assets		5.6
7. Avg. Collection	1. Sales per Day 2. Receivables / Sales/Day		37 Days
8. Inventory Turnover	Net Sales / Inventory		17.9
9. Fixed Assets to Tangible N.W.			60%
10. Debt to Equity	Total Debt / Net Worth		56%
11. Profit Margin	Net Profit / Net Sales		4.2%
12. Return on Assets	Net Profit / Assets		14%
13. Return on Investment	Net Profit / Net Worth		21%
14. COGS %	COGS / Net Sales		48%
15. Fixed Assets to Working Capital			2.21%

Figure 5.21 *A sample budget report using percentages and ratios.*

* *Annual Statement Studies,* Robert Morris Assoc., Philadelphia Bank Building, Philadelphia, PA 19107.

Miscellaneous. The sky and your imagination are the limits to what else you can do. This miscellaneous category might include pension fund, insurance, breakeven calculations, production scheduling, job costing, new product cost analysis, loan amortization, buy-versus-lease comparison, discounted cash flow (DCF)—net present value, taxes of all kinds, property management, or special packages unique to particular businesses.

Word Processing (WP)

WP may be the most rapidly growing area within the computer field at the present. There is a good chance that if you purchase a small computer from an established company, you will find several WP packages available for it. In the next few years data processing (DP) and WP will move into a combined approach and the WP portion will become more standardized. Right now, many software firms have introduced WP systems with little or no thought to uniformity within the industry or user requirements. A shakedown will occur in WP, the same way that it has in other portions of computer-related applications. Even though there is rapid change in the field, we do not recommend that you let this deter you from getting into the use of WP, especially some of the simpler packages such as letter writing and mailing list maintenance. WP should be a very real consideration when you are looking at a computer. The WP equipment on the market ranges from memory typewriters to entire systems, costing thousands and thousands of dollars, that approach the automated office concept. Unless there is an excellent reason in your business to do so, you should not consider purchasing DP and WP equipment separately. The newer small computers combine these functions both internally (with programs) and externally (through the keyboard).

Individual characters, words, sentences, and entire reports are treated like other types of information by a computer. WP is essentially a subset of DP, if you consider "data" to be all kinds of information. Probably one of the first widely available commercial machines that made a major breakthrough in WP was IBM's Magnetic Tape Selectric Typewriter (MTST). The machine stored pages of information on tape cartridges and allowed an operator to make corrections to the body of a letter or a report without having to do a lot of retyping. Repetitive letters that were typed automatically could be sent out with all the look of a hand-typed document.

The capabilities of modern WP systems are becoming nothing short of phenomenal. You should be certain that you know what the WP package will do for you and your business. If you never write letters, reports, or plans and do not plan to do any direct mail advertising or sales, then posssibly WP is not something that you can effectively take advantage of at this time.

If you are looking into WP, be certain that you are also looking into the kind of printer that will serve your needs. For example, if you plan to send out multiple letters and you want them to appear as if they had been individually typed, be aware that not all printers print like a typewriter. The cheaper printers use 5-by-7 dot matrix patterns similar to those described in Chapter 2, and the reader can tell at a glance that a computer, not your secretary, wrote the letter. In addition, some computer programs for WP have terrible inflexibilities: A man whose name is George Appleton III may occasionally receive a computer-prepared letter which starts "Dear Mr. III."

WP's major task these days is devoted to text handling—combining the power of a computer with that of an automatic typewriter. A good WP system will allow you to do some of the following things with written material:

- Create and justify both left and right margins.
- Fix errors of all kinds; insert a phrase in the body of the text; and change the format of the entire document.
- Add or delete characters, lines, or paragraphs.
- Move entire paragraphs to different parts of the text.
- Use different type fonts and styles within the text.
- Number pages automatically.
- Insert special text.
- Date automatically.
- Compose letters by selecting any number of standard paragraphs from a master file that contains a large number of paragraphs.
- Create mailing labels.

As time goes by, the capabilities of WP will be enlarged and expanded and it will move more closely to DP until both areas become one. There is already some overlap. The dunning letters ("pay up or else") that are part of a standard A/P package are more a part of WP than DP.

Data File Management

At some point, you may need a computer program to help you manage files of information. A file is any collection of individual records that are grouped together by some title or classification. For example, a list of all your customers, together with address, telephone, name of customer contact, types of items purchased, previous year's purchases, is a *customer file*. These records are usually grouped together on some recording medium like a floppy or hard disk. Your operating system may not be as capable as you want for handling data on a file. One package, available for most small computers and compatible with operating systems such as CP/M described in Chapter 3, is called "Microfile" and is available from PRS-The Program of the Month. To use the program, your computer must be equipped with a Z-80 or 8080 series microprocessor and must have a minimum of 16K of random access memory. Although the program has a variety of features to help you maintain, access, and analyze data files, the following represent the major tasks that Microfile will perform:

- Addition of a record to an already existing file.
- Editing of an existing record (the address change of a customer, for example).
- Deletion of a record.
- Searching for a record or a collection of records.
- Justification of columns, both left and right.
- Sorting (ordering) either upwards or downwards by any attribute like Zip code.
- Listing of the file either on the CRT (soft copy) or the printer (hard copy).
- Formatting the output—an example of this capability would be to list all customers, alphabetically by name, with space between the alphabetic groups (A,B,C).
- Computing of column totals. You might want to see the total of sales of all customers in a particular state, for example.

A complete, descriptive manual is available at no charge by writing to PRS, 257 Central Park West, New York, NY 10024.

Summary

The importance of the computer in small business is a well established fact. Over the next ten to twenty years, hundreds of thousands of machines will be sold to business owners who operate every conceivable kind of venture. Both hardware and software will tend to become more standardized. The software is the key to the successful operation of your computer. Some reminders that we have stressed before are:

- Be certain that the software closely emulates your own operation. Although changes in your business are going to occur, you want these to be held to a minimum.
- Learn as much as you can about the software package before you purchase it.
- Keep the cost down—don't get sold a package that isn't cost-effective.
- Be sure that the software you choose runs on the machine that you select.
- Choose the software first, the machine second.
- See the software that you are seriously considering being used in another small business that resembles yours as closely as possible.
- Learn as much programming as you can without diverting your attention from other parts of your business.
- Keep an eye on new developments. Don't be afraid to change when it is called for, don't change things that are working fine, and learn to recognize the difference between the two.

We will use some of the material developed in this chapter for the analysis presented in Chapter 6—how to justify a computer financially.

Chapter 6 Justifying a Computer for Your Business

About twenty years ago, large businesses began to look on the computer as a tool that could help management and operational decision-making rather than as a machine which was limited to scientific calculations. The machines of that era were capable of handling business problems. COBOL was available, and applications software were becoming readily available. The decision to analyze the conversion from manual or punched-card operation to full EDP usually began with something known as a "feasibility study." Now, you would suspect that an EDP feasibility study would carefully assess an organization's problems and opportunities in relation to the available computer hardware and software, personnel skills, costs, physical requirements, projected savings, and a host of other things and then arrive at a mathematically justified conclusion as to whether the organization should have a computer *or not*. Note the emphasis on the last two words. The studies were not supposed to have any bias, but nearly every one of them did—in favor of the computer. I have never seen a "feasibility study" that recommended against buying or leasing a computer. The consistent result of the studies is no surprise when you look at the table below:

Who Did the Study?	*What Was in the Back of Their Minds?*
1. A machine manufacturer	1. Sale or rental of a machine (theirs!)
2. An outside consultant	2. More consulting or auditing work
3. Inside employees	3. Job justification

The feasibility studies were, in fact, intended to prepare the organization for the computer by getting people to think about the device in a positive way. IBM loved this approach and capitalized on it brilliantly. There was no inherent "evil" in what they (and others) did; it was just plain good business sense. The point of this brief discussion is to prepare you to do your own feasibility study in a logical way—but remember that there's no getting around the fact that computers are just plain fun.

Advantages of the Small Computer

- They are exceedingly fast, reliable, and accurate.
- Computers can store all the data you could conceivably come up with and recall it with ease.
- Unlike their big brothers and sisters, the new machines do not require special environmental considerations such as 440-volt, three-phase power, a raised floor (for cables), or air conditioning.
- Your basic decision-making process will be improved due to more timely information.
- If you wisely analyze the purchase and balance cost with performance, you will save money in the long run.
- Your personal knowledge will be increased.
- They're fun, and they give status.

Disadvantages of the Small Computer

- Like anything else in the world, they have limitations. They will not "save" a business that is predestined to fail. They can't think.
- It means a personal commitment on your part or on the part of your people. You must learn something about them.
- It will cost you money and the savings may be a long time in coming.
- When a computer burps or hiccups, it can make one whale of a mistake.
- There are hidden costs that you will not see at the outset.

- Your first computer may not be the one you stay with (Smith's Law #41).
- At one time or another, you will be tempted to take a chain saw to it.

Calculating Cost Savings

Your decision to purchase a computer should be based, in part, on a strict business analysis. The net benefit should accrue directly to the business in terms of increased profit–it's that simple. The ultimate cost of the computer has more than a casual relationship with the size of your business in terms of annual net sales. Figure 6.1 is a graph of the relationship between these two variables. The graph is not precise, and shouldn't be taken as gospel. It's an estimate based on our observations of computer use by businesses of different sizes.

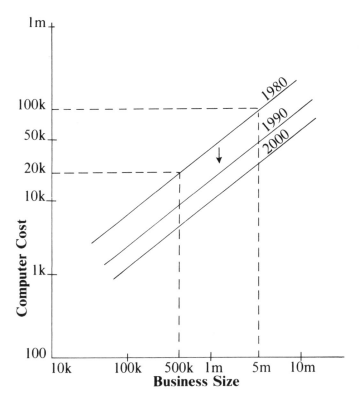

Figure 6.1 *The relationship between computer cost and business size.*

Some businesses need a computer more than others. Many grocery and hardware stores, for example, have their inventory, purchasing, and accounts payable done by their suppliers for little or no cost, and that is a very real consideration.

In these two brief examples, we will take into consideration the cost of the computer system itself (that is, the hardware) and will ignore the cost of software and maintenance because these are judgmental items. You may program the machine yourself and even take care of the maintenance. These two costs, if incurred, will probably be offset by such intangible savings as accuracy and timeliness.

Example 1

Many small-business owners have developed a rule of thumb about having their own computer—it should save one clerical person. With this in mind, the cost analysis becomes easy. For example, one clerical person receives wages of $5.00 an hour which includes wage-mandated payments (employer's share of FICA, federal and state unemployment taxes, workman's compensation insurance), and benefits (vacation, holidays, medical and life insurance). The annual cost of that employee is $10,400 ($5.00/hr × 40 hrs/wk × 52 wks/yr). The next part of the problem is to decide the time period over which the analysis should take place, or, in the words of a financial analyst, the payback period.

Some entrepreneurs will keep their computer for a year or even less, give it to the kids, and buy a bigger one; others may keep it ten years or longer. Let's take two and one-half years as a probable economic "life" of the machine. The actual period is probably much longer, but it's better to stay conservative on this analysis. The most that someone in our example of a "saving-of-one-person" analysis should pay, then, is $26,000 (2.5 × $10,400).

Example 2

Other entrepreneurs tell us that they plan no personnel change at all and want to see an actual analysis of the cost saving by application. This is a bit risky, but as long as you understand and can deal with the assumptions that are made, the financial analysis can be rather accurate.

In doing this analysis, we are going to stick with the major applications presented in Chapter 5: general ledger, accounts payable, accounts receivable, inventory control, and payroll. Inventory control is really the key item since the cost savings in the other four can be small by comparison.

General Ledger. Most accountants are simply assemblers of numbers and the computer can do this faster and more accurately than they can. But before you call your bean-counter and tell him or her what to do with their debits and credits, remember that good accountants give advice, interpret regulations, and analyze final information—things the computer isn't yet able to do. A computer won't replace your accountant, but can reduce his or her work load—and charges to you.

Accounts Payable. The name of the game with payables is to delay them as long as good business sense dictates. Cash retained is cash used. But there is an opposite side to payables. Some suppliers are adamant about being paid on or before a certain date. If you fail to pay them (even though it may be an honest error on your part) they can shut you off. No supplies, no sales. No sales, no money. Business goes belly-up.

Accounts Receivable. If you do not use normal credit arrangements, this category may not pertain to you. If you do extend credit, then you should do everything you can to collect these receivables quickly. The computer can handle the entire receivables aging process and can send letters for you. It can even keep a record of poor credit risks.

Inventory Control. As we said before, this area is the real key. Outside of any fixed assets like real estate and equipment, here is where most of your business really is. The name of the inventory game is to hold only movable, salable, profitable items but never to run out of an item that a customer might need. Among other things, inventory control includes:

- Economic Order Quantity: a mathematical technique which calculates the lowest inventory costs as a function of the costs of ordering and the costs of storing the inventory (floor or shelf space cost, insurance and so on).
- Analyzing slow-moving items and removing them, if desirable.
- Calculating the gross or net profit on each item of inventory.

Some small businesses have claimed a dollar savings of one-half of their average annual inventory level, but this is certainly the exception and not the rule.

Payroll. In olden times, circa 1965, a large company might purchase a $2 million computer, hire a trainload of computer people, build a special room, and spend another fortune on supplies and maintenance. At the end of one year, the only thing that they had to show for all this was a program to do payroll. The company spent several megabucks to replace two or three $100-a-week payroll clerks. Not very smart. Don't expect to save a lot with a payroll program directly, but remember all the garbage that you have to send to the feds.

Let's do a brief calculation based on some assumptions. (You can crank your own numbers in to reflect your business.) This hypothetical business has the following characteristics:

Sales:	$ 300,000
Average Inventory:	$ 90,000
Average Accounts Payable:	$ 20,000
Average Accounts Receivable:	$ 30,000
Number of Employees:	5
Annual Accounting Charges:	$ 2,000
Owner's Compensation:	$ 25,000

Table 6.1 presents an analysis of potential annual savings based on the above figures.

TABLE 6.1

Cost Savings Example

Item	Projected Effect	Annual Savings
General Ledger	Annual accounting charges will be cut in half.	$ 1,000
Accounts Payable	The net effect of savings will be 1% of the average payables.	200
Accounts Receivable	Net effect is 2% of receivables.	600
Inventory	A 5% saving.	4,500
Payroll	A saving of $1.00 per employee per week ($1 × 5 × 52).	260
Owner's Time	The computer will "save" two hours of the owner's time per week to release him or her for more profitable tasks. ($25,000 ÷ 2080 hrs/yr × 2 hrs/wk × 50 wks/yr.)	1,200
TOTAL ESTIMATED ANNUAL SAVINGS		$ 7,760

Using the 2.5 year figure as before, our hypothetical business should spend no more than $19,400 for the machine and its software.

You can do your own analysis by using Figure 6.2 as a worksheet.

Business_____

Date_____

Item	Value to be Used	Space for Assumptions and Calculations	Estimated Annual Savings
General Ledger	$_____		$_____
Payables	$_____		_____
Receivables	$_____		_____
Inventory	$_____		_____
Payroll	_____emp.		_____
Owner	$_____		_____
Other			_____
TOTAL ESTIMATED ANNUAL SAVINGS			$_____

Figure 6.2 *My business.*

Financial Analysis

Before leaving this chapter behind, we should do a very brief financial analysis. Let us assume that:

- An entrepreneur buys a new computer for $20,000. The IRS allows the device to be depreciated over three years on a sum-of-the-years'-digits basis.
- The business's tax rate is 20 percent of net profit.

- It is estimated that the computer will save $8000 per year in directly recognizable costs.
- Inflation is 10 percent per year.

The analysis is shown in Table 6.2.

TABLE 6.2

Computer Purchase Financial Analysis

1	2	3 (2 × 20%)	4	5 (3 + 4)	6	7 (5 ÷ 6)
Year	Total Annual Depreciation	Tax Effect of Depreciation	Cost Saving	Total Saving	10% Deflation Factor	Final Discounted Saving
1	$10,000(³⁄₆)	$2,000	$ 8,000	$10,000	1.100	$ 9,091
2	6,667(²⁄₆)	1,333	8,000	9,333	1.210	7,713
3	3,333(¹⁄₆)	667	8,000	8,667	1.331	6,512
	$20,000(⁶⁄₆)	$4,000	$24,000	$28,000		$23,316

Less: Initial Investment − 20,000

Net Discounted Savings $ 3,316

The total savings figure of $28,000 in column five is equivalent to an annualized rate of return over three years of 20 percent on the $20,000 investment. NOTE: You will need a *computer* to do the rate of return calculation.

I think that everything in Table 6.2 is relatively self-explanatory except the deflation factor (column six) and its effect on final discounted saving (column seven). For this example, we said that the inflation rate was going to be 10 percent. That means that $1.00 in the beginning of a year with 10 percent inflation is worth only about 91¢ at the end of that year ($1.00 ÷ 1.10). At the end of the second year, the dollar will have declined to 83¢, and so on. If inflation is running at a different level, 18 percent for example, the divisor becomes 1.18.

In our example, the $20,000 was spent in "Year 0" and did not produce the savings of $10,000 (column five) until the end of the year, therefore we must reduce that $10,000 to get it into "today's" dollars.

The problem with all this analysis is that one $20,000 computer is essentially just like another. However, although the hardware may perform the same basic functions, there are other things to consider before making a final purchase. These are covered in Chapter 7.

Chapter 7 Evaluating and Selecting a Computer System

We are not going to make comparisons between available hardware since this area seems to change from day to day. Manufacturers of small computers and peripheral equipment seem to come and go on a regular basis. If you want to get the latest information on computer availability, visit a few of the retail computer outlets. Check the Yellow Pages under "Data Processing Systems, Equipment, and Supplies" and make a few phone calls. After a week, you will have enough sales literature to fill your clothes closet. And—you'll be thoroughly confused. Everyone will claim that their company's machine outperforms the competition. That's mostly hogwash. By and large, the machines in the same general price category are also somewhat similar in what they do. One machine has a blue keyboard whereas their competitor uses black. The printer from company A has a stand to hold it; company B's printer sits on a table. And so on.

Probably the biggest single test in evaluating a computer system is to visit someone who has been using the machine that you are considering. Talk to them. Ask questions:

- Were the salespeople cooperative, reliable, and helpful?
- Did the machine cost what you expected or were there hidden expenses that you hadn't anticipated? What were they?
- What, if anything, went wrong early in the process?

- What are the good points about this machine? The manufacturer?
- If you could have known one thing about computers before you started all this, what would it have been?
- What has the software support been like?
- Has the machine broken down often? How was it fixed? How long did it stay broken? Who repaired it?
- Did the computer save money or did it create more work?
- Is the machine still big enough or have you outgrown it?
- What else can you tell me?
- Would you do it again? (Most important!)

Getting firsthand input from someone who has been through the computer mill beats all the sales puffery and nonsense that you'll have to dig through to get meaningful information for your decision. There are about 150 manufacturers of various types of computer systems and peripherals and the analysis of the "right" machine can become staggering. Although this chapter cannot answer all your questions, it will give you a kind of road map through the computer jungle. The Notepad for Computer Evaluation in Appendix B provides a convenient format for evaluating any hardware you look at. Copy the pages and take the copies with you to fill out as you examine potential systems and talk to the people who sell them.

The Manufacturer/Vendor

You don't have the time to deal with everyone in the racket, or at least, you shouldn't. Your business is the single most important thing in your life and it needs tending to first and foremost. Don't become obsessed with computer evaluation to the detriment of day-to-day operation. On the other hand, if you're really serious about a computing system, it's not a light decision. Selecting a vendor presents a dilemma. The manufacturers who have been around for a while have experience in the technology and the market. Their names— IBM, Control Data, Minneapolis-Honeywell, Univac, NCR, Burroughs, Digital Equipment, Data General, Wang, Hewlett-Packard, Texas Instrument, Pertec—are household words. They are large, reputable firms with an established track record in engineering, production, marketing, service, and (not the least of all) financial stability. They have proven to the world that they can pull through recessions and downturns. There are drawbacks to using these firms, however:

- These firms may not be in a position to give you much personal service. The sale of a $15,000 computer by a company in the billion-dollar sales club doesn't even pay for one receptionist at one of their plants.
- Some of these giants fail to design their equipment from the market up. One

large manufacturer, for example, sells a computer that cannot easily be programmed. Too often, the big companies feel that you should buy their equipment because they designed it. Their size becomes somewhat self-defeating.

• Because of their size, these companies may have staggering overhead costs, and this can be reflected in the price of their equipment. (NOTE: This is sometimes balanced by the fact that they are producing small computers in large volume and can pass the volume economy on to you.)

We are a land of free enterprise and we love to root for the little guy. Sometimes the smaller, newer vendor may offer a better machine—and better service as well. The real problem here is one of staying power. If the supplier has been in business for less than five years and has less than $10 million in annual sales, the next recession may put the business under.

Regardless of what you do, consider these questions before making your final decision:

• How long has the manufacturer been in business? Are they making a good profit?
• Does the manufacturer make a complete system (input device, CPU, output device, random access memory) or only one part? If they offer only a CPU, for example, where do you go for your CRT/keyboard, flexible disk unit, and printer? Is this a problem or an opportunity?
• What kind of training and support documentation does the vendor offer? Is it an extra cost?
• Does the manufacturer support the equipment with service or must you go to someone else?
• Is systems and application software available from the manufacturer?
• Who installs the machine?
• What are the general warranty terms?
• Who is responsible for seeing that the entire system operates the way it is supposed to?
• What are the "hidden" costs?
• Is computer sales and service the primary function of the supplier or just a side business?
• Will the vendor commit costs and delivery schedule to writing?

Maintenance

With today's smaller computers, maintenance is not the problem that it once was. It's quite conceivable that the electronics may operate for centuries without repair. The mechanical gizmos—print heads and wheels, ribbon and paper feeds, disk drive mechanisms and the like—will wear out or break, but even some of these are simple to fix. The fewer mechanical elements, though, the less maintenance is required. Maintenance by the supplier is not a necessity (unless so stated in the purchase or lease contract or warranty) but be damn certain that you know who will do it and how much it will cost. Since the first major breakdown will occur the day after the warranty expires (Smith's Law # 16), you should know that maintenance can be done two ways:

- A contract: It's basically an insurance policy. You pay a certain amount every month which covers all service work. The monthly charges may increase somewhat after about the fifth year and if you keep the machine for ten years or more, you may reach the point where no one will maintain it.
- Time and materials. You pay as you go, just like auto repair. This is akin to self-insurance.

When your computer is in the shop, you don't have the use of it. Some companies can get you a "loaner" if the machine is to be out of service for a while, but this may be rare. One thing that's always baffled me: computer peddlers wax loquacious about how reliable their equipment is. But just before you sign on the dotted line, they whip out an involved and expensive maintenance contract. Well, friend, which is it?

Software

There are two kinds of software:

Systems Software: programming instructions which tell the machine what to do with itself—operating systems, compilers, interpreters, or utility programs (sort, **merge**, select).
Applications Software: program packages which do actual tasks—payroll, general ledger accounting, or inventory control.

The systems software should be supplied by the manufacturer. Some of it is internal to the machine, contained in read-only memory (ROM) and some of it is external, on floppy or hard disks or on cassette or cartridge tapes. One manufacturer suggests that the systems software have multiple-use capability. This is only important if you need access to the machine while it is working on something else.

For instance, suppose it is a few days beyond the close of your accounting period and the computer is assimilating all the period's accounting data in preparation for producing financial statements. A customer calls in with an order for two dozen yards of red velvet so you want to use the computer for your perpetual inventory. With a **multiprocessing** capability, you can inquire directly without bothering the accounting program. Otherwise, you will have to wait until the program finishes, interrupt it, or go look in the yards goods section yourself.

The machine supplier may or may not offer applications packages; this really is not important. You'll pay for them regardless. As we said before, there are thousands of software houses that offer prepared programs or the capability to adapt an existing program to your needs or prepare a special one from scratch.

Some considerations about software packages:

- What do they cost? Is there a "maintenance" charge as well? NOTE: the payment of a monthly maintenance charge assures you of getting all new changes to the program—for example, new federal withholding rates for the payroll program.
- How much documentation is provided?
- Is the language either BASIC or COBOL? If not, why not?
- Is the language interactive in nature; that is does the program "talk" to you?
- Do the packages represent industry-accepted methods of calculation and data presentation?
- What error routines and messages are included? For instance, when entering an address does the program confirm that the state and the Zip code match?
- Do the programs require that some minimum hardware feature, such as internal memory, be satisfied? The following hardware configuration is required for the general accounting and word processing software for a major software supplier: "Any 8080, Z-80, or 8085 microcomputer with a 132-column printer, video unit, two flexible disk units (minimum 0.5 megabyte on-line), and 48K bytes of RAM (Random Access Memory)."
- Does the software have a warranty period?

Hardware

The following was adapted from "A Guide to Evaluating Small Business Systems," which is available free of charge from Data General Corporation, Westboro, Massachusetts 01581. Unlike much other sales literature, the brochure is informative, well-done, and reasonably objective.

Central Processing Unit (CPU)

- How much memory does the CPU hold? Is it sufficient to handle the programs you will run?
- Can more memory be added after system installation?
- Does the CPU include an automatic restart capability in case of power loss?
- Can sections of one program be protected from unauthorized access?

- Can the CPU be protected from unauthorized access (i.e., does it have a lock and key; can a password scheme be easily implemented)?
- What type of electrical power does the CPU require? Can it easily be installed in your environment?

In general, small business system CPU's are fast enough to handle any business function you require. Look for a CPU with more memory capability than you may need initially, so the system can expand as your business grows. A memory protection capability is important, whether there are multiple users or a need to limit access of pertinent information to authorized personnel. Also, some CPU's require a special environment in which to operate effectively; this is very rare in today's small computers and unless there is a strong reason to the contrary, you should not consider a machine that requires this kind of special treatment.

Data Storage Files

The most important consideration for a mass storage (external memory) unit is its capacity, based on the amount of information you need stored now—as well as your projected growth. The vendor can give you record size estimates to help you determine storage requirements.

Data storage files, as we mentioned earlier, are usually available in two forms—floppy disks and hard disks. Diskette (floppy disk) storage, used for smaller volumes of data, is measured in hundreds of thousands of characters of information. Hard disks, which hold large volumes of data, are measured in megabytes (millions of characters of information).

- Does the system support diskettes, hard disks, or both types of data storage? Do you need both?
- How many diskettes can be used at once? Two? Four? Eight?
- How many million characters (megabytes) do the hard disks hold?
- What is the maximum amount of data storage the system will support?
- Can data storage units be added at any time after system installation? How many? At what price?

In general, a small business system should offer a broad enough range of mass storage capabilities so your business will not outgrow your system. Floppy and hard disks combined—if they are part of the initial system·configuration—will make data backup and copying simple and inexpensive. Otherwise, it is an additional expense. Incompatibility problems are reduced if all mass storage units are from a single vendor or manufacturer.

Hard disks are the most efficient data storage units available for small business systems. These disks provide the highest storage capacity and the fastest access to stored data. On a cost-per-stored-byte basis, they are usually the least expensive input/output device.

Diskette drives (floppies) are the least expensive data storage device. Diskettes are sturdy enough for mail travel (in special envelopes) making them ideal for transporting data between computer sites. Diskettes, however, have a shorter usable lifetime than hard disks. Most small computers that use floppies have a built-in routine which tells you when to replace a floppy disk that may have become worn. You copy the older disk onto a new one and throw the old one away.

Workstation

This is usually a keyboard coupled up with a CRT. The workstation is an important system component that lets you or your employees enter, inquire, update, examine and modify information in any computer-stored file. Requests and modifications are made on a typewriter-like keyboard, and the operator watches the transaction on the video screen. Questions to ask include:

- How many workstations can the system support?
- Can workstations be added at any time after system installation?
- How many characters can be displayed on the screen at one time? (A 24-line by 80-character configuration is minimum.)
- Can the workstation be located far enough from the computer to suit your needs?
- Does each workstation require its own specially designed desk or table?
- Is a 10-key numeric (adding machine) keypad standard or optional?

Look for operator-comfort features that reduce physical strain, such as swivel and tilt screens, movable keyboards and brightness controls. If a workstation must sit on a specially designed desk or table, check for hidden costs—the special units should be part of the system package.

Printers

As we said earlier, two types of printers are available with most small business systems. The type and speed you need is best determined by the frequency and amount of printed transaction copies you require. Character printers print one character at a time, and line printers print an entire line at a time. Character printers are slower but much less expensive than line printers, and may produce high quality output. Line printers are used for high-speed report production. The following are important:

- Can the system support more than one printer at the same time?
- How fast do the character printers operate?
- How fast do the line printers operate?

- What operator features are available?
- How far from the computer can a printer be located?
- Can the printer provide hard copy of data displayed on a CRT?
- Can the printer operate simultaneously with a workstation?
- Can a printer be added at any time after system installation?
- Does the printer provide upper and lower case characters? (This is important in word processing.)
- Can the printer provide multiple copies? Will it fit your forms? What about checks?

In general, look for a small business system that includes a printer. The word "optional" usually means you have to spend more money. Ideally, the vendor should offer a variety of printers—different speeds and types—so you can choose the one that best meets your requirements. Look for a range of character features—upper-case and lower-case letters, underscoring, and punctuation marks generally improve report quality and readability.

Sometimes printers are used as workstations, giving printed output instead of video. Printer workstations are slower and are generally used in specialized applications that require immediate documentation.

Is the machine *batch* or *interactive?* With a batch machine, you load a job, run it, get the results—one job at a time. If you have new data, you must run the job again. An interactive machine can process a run sometimes with only the entry of a few pieces of data.

Money

The computer and everything associated with it will cost you money. As we pointed out in Chapter 6, it should save you money in the long run. If it doesn't, forget it as a business investment, although you may rationalize some of the purchase as an educational experience. Some of the hidden costs associated with a computer are:

- insurance
- installation—physical changes, new room, power cables
- energy consumption
- all kinds of supplies, including backup files
- training time; possible personnel addition
- interest on borrowed money
- future changes and additions

These additional costs are not usually large, but you should be aware that the expense of having a computer goes beyond simply the machine and its programs. In addition, if you are like most other small business owners with a computer, it will take you longer to get the machine fully operative in your business than you initially thought it would.

Rent, Lease, or Buy?

Table 7.1 presents some basic differences between the three alternatives.

TABLE 7.1

Ownership Comparison

Item	Rent	Lease	Buy
Ownership (who owns it)	Vendor	Vendor or third party but may revert to you at end of lease period	You
Term	Month-to-month	1–5 years	Indefinite
Relative expense to you	Highest	Moderate	Least
Returnability period	60 days (written notice)	End of lease or with cancellation charge	N/A
Usual accounting treatment	Expense	Mixed (see your accountant)	Capital expenditure—depreciation and investment tax credit available
Major disadvantage	Cost	Locked in to lease period	Little recourse to supplier

When you are coming close to a final decision on the equipment you need, you should do a cost analysis of renting, leasing, and buying that equipment to see which alternative makes most sense. Note that in leasing computers, as in leasing other equipment, the "Rule of 40" seems to hold as a guideline. That is, if the leased machine has a price tag of $20,000, the monthly lease charge will be around $500 ($20,000 ÷ 40).

Chapter 8 Planning for the Computer

One nice thing about most small computers is that you can go out and buy one, stick it in the trunk of your car, bring it to your business, plug it in, and *voilà!* Instant computership! Whether you spend a few grand or a few hundred grand, a little forethought and planning will help you through the transition period—which can last a few days or a few years—and into the fully operational phase and beyond. The following list does not include everything but should get you thinking about the implementation of data processing.

- Where are you going to put the machine? Ideally, it will have its own little corner away from the mainstream of other activities. If the computer has more than one terminal, are the remote terminals close to the point where the initial data to be fed to it originates?
- Based upon the recommendations of the manufacturer, are there any environmental considerations such as temperature, humidity, dust, or power that should be reckoned with? Even though small computers plug directly into the wall (and some have a battery backup for emergencies), it's a good idea to have a "dedicated" circuit for the computer. You don't want someone to use an electric toothbrush on the same line and cause the machine to sneeze and lose things.
- Who will be the principal operator of the machine? You? Is that smart? After all, you are the all-wise, all-seeing entrepreneur and should not be spending all day slaving over a hot keyboard. Maybe it's better to have Harry or Suzy trained to run it, although you should learn the system as well.

- Have you really thought through your total business operation? What really happens to information as it is (a) created by something like a sale or an inventory purchase, (b) processed by you, or a cash register, or a bank, and (c) presented in the form of a report like an inventory count? Have you analyzed the business transactions and the data flow in your operation?
- Have you *written down* a time schedule of important events such as delivery of the computer, initial debugging and testing phase, first application completed and running? This data processing plan is most crucial to your successful and profitable implementation.
- In what order are you going to convert from manual to outside service preparation to automated processing? Does it make sense? Most small businesses go for payroll first since it's usually the easiest.
- Have you thought through the next two or three years of your business? What will growth do to your computer?
- Have you made a list of reports—both as-needed and periodic—that you will eventually require?
- If the computer gets too small too quickly, can your programs operate with little or no change on a larger machine?

One strong word of caution about the importance of knowing where you are going with regard to the computer: It is very possible to get to a stage of near-chaos with a computer. This informationally anarchistic state has two simultaneously occurring characteristics:

Characteristic A: So many programs have been developed and tied into other programs that the entire process becomes 90 percent worthless, but it is too late to back down without destroying everything. Be sure that any new program is fully justified before it is begun and be also sure to release any programs that are no longer useful.

Characteristic B: The computer changes its role from slave to master. The business can no longer function unless the computer functions.

Many large businesses are at a very critical stage right now because of layer upon layer of interlocking programs. The entire system has been made tenuous by this perilous hierarchy. No one human being, or even a team of them, can reassemble this software Humpty Dumpty. I predict that in the next decade a number of large institutions will reach a "critical mass" in processing and some nice morning the entire thing will implode in a huge heap of zero's and one's.

Somebody will just have to start over.

Before you make your final commitment, be certain that you have gone as far as you can in your investigation of suppliers of both hardware and software. One very basic consideration beyond the financial justification is whether you want the machine or not. Don't forget, discount, or by-pass your intuition.

As a part of your pre-purchase activities, you should look at several machines and several applications packages and develop an idea of which hardware/software combination is the best for your business. You should make a number of visits to computer retail stores and you should have a few computer salespeople stop by your business. You should also see a number of computer systems in operation, read a book like this one (and possibly one other), and attend a seminar or two. In other words, be sure that you are as ready as you can be.

The plan to computerize should be just as well prepared and thought through as your business plan. You don't have a business plan, you say? Then you should buy a copy of *How to Prosper in Your Own Business* published by The Stephen Greene Press.

Chapter 9 Final Thoughts

Now that you've made it this far, congratulations. Whether you realize it or not, your knowledge of electronic data processing is now quite substantial: You know what a computer is (and isn't); how we got to where we are today with computers; how these infernal machines work; what you can do with them; and whether they make sense for your business. In Appendix A we will take out our crystal ball and look into the future to try to give you some idea of what's coming in the next twenty-five years. But before we propel you forward there are a few matters that should be covered to round out your "education."

Alternatives to the Computer

Maybe a computer is really not for you and your business. This, of course, sounds like pure heresy and would cause any DP salesperson to come and let the air out of my tires, but it might be true. Possibly your business is too small. Maybe you really can "carry it in your head." Maybe, between your suppliers and your accountant, you really get all the things you need. And don't discount your emotions, either. They are very powerful and, in many cases, the feeling from the heart is far more persuasive than the logic from the head. If you decide against your own machine now, just remember that a year from now may bring a totally different picture. And keep in mind that every fact, every reason always has (like a coin) an obverse side. A supplier who processes the information about your inventory controls your inventory and the information about it. Is that what you want? Does that make sense from an audit trial standpoint?

Other than manual data processing (pencil, paper, calculator, cash register), there are three alternate routes available to you:

- *A Programmable Calculator.* For prices ranging from $25 to $500 you can buy almost-a-computer. These devices are really marvelous and, properly used, can solve some rather involved problems. They can't handle large amounts of data, however.
- *Time Sharing.* In this case, you rent a terminal (usually a keyboard/printer device like the Teletype machine) that is connected by a normal long-distance telephone line to a large computer in some other location, maybe a hundred miles away. You can safely store all your data on the big computer and then operate on it whenever you want. The only real problem nowadays is cost. Years ago, when a total computer would have set you back $100,000 or so, time sharing was viable. With $15,000 machines around, that isn't so true any more. With time sharing, you will have both fixed and variable expenses. Fixed expenses include a minimum monthly charge from the DP center, and rent and maintenance on the terminal. Variable expenses include long-distance telephone charges, connect time to the computer, a transmission charge depending upon the number of characters sent and received, and a storage charge for files kept by the computer. You can plan on time sharing costing from $200 to $2000 per month, depending on your usage.
- *Service Bureaus.* A DP service bureau is simply a company that is in business to provide you with programming and computer support. Usually they have programs already prepared for things like payroll and receivables. You bring your work to them, or they pick it up, do the processing, and bill you for it. You pay as you go. If you have a service bureau prepare a program for you, be certain that you own the program and that it is compatible with most small computers. The best way to find out the costs involved is to ask a reputable house to come in and make a proposal to you.

Used Equipment

I have only one word of advice regarding the purchase of used computers: Don't! A true story follows. In the late 1960's I was called to the corporate headquarters of one of the nation's ten largest life insurance companies in New York City. After some preliminaries, the data processing director proudly announced that he had just purchased two IBM 7080 computers at an auction. He only paid $100,000 each. A bargain, right? A bargain, wrong! It was true that these ten-year-old machines had cost a couple of million new and were in perfect working order . . . *but* there was a major problem beyond the physical age of the hardware.

Our conversation went something like this:

> ME: Harry, that's a great price, Do you have room for them?
> HIM: Yeah. The whole fifth floor.
> ME: What about air conditioning, humidity control, and a space for the tape library?
> HIM: No problem.
> ME: Will IBM maintain them?
> HIM: Yeah. For the next five years at least, maybe longer. And the cost isn't bad either.
> ME: Who's going to program them?
> HIM: My people. Why?
> ME: Harry, what language does the 7080 use?
> HIM: Autocoder. I cut my teeth on it.
> ME: What primary language does your programming staff use?
> *(Pause)*
> HIM: COBOL. . . . Oh, my God!

Sure, he knew Autocoder and so did a lot of other people but the people that knew Autocoder were now highly paid DP managers. The younger staff didn't know Autocoder from Swahili. He would be in the same fix as a Latin teacher trying to revive a dead language. The training costs and lost time would be phenomenal.

Documentation

If you buy software packages, the supplier will give you documentation with the programs. If you write a program yourself, you will do the documentation—or you'd better, if you don't want to get into lots of trouble later.

Each set of documentation for a program should be in a separate notebook section or manila folder labeled with the name of the program and the latest revision. The contents of this file are up to you. A suggested format:

1. Title Page
   a. name of program
   b. date prepared
   c. level and date of latest revision
   d. machine used
   e. language used
2. Revision Page (example shown in Figure 9.1)

Page: 1 of 1
___

PROGRAM: PAYROLL 1

DATE FIRST PREPARED: 12/4/XX   BY: B.R. Smith

MACHINE: Unimicrodata 4500

LANGUAGE: BASIC III

___

REVISION	DATE	CHANGE	INITIALS
A	12/4/xx	Initial preparation and run.	---
B	1/17/x1	Withholding rates changed to reflect latest IRS regulations.	---
C	2/27/x1	Line 01720 changed from "LET WITH = $W^*.29^*C$" to "LET WITH =$W^*.31^*C$".	---

Figure 9.1 *Revision schedule for program documentation.*

3. Written Program Description
    a. introduction
    b. purpose
    c. special files used
    d. processing
    e. output
    f. language used
    g. other programs affected
4. Flow Chart of Program
5. Special Operating Instructions
    a. peripheral equipment needed
    b. switch setting on console
6. Diagnostic Routines Used
    a. error checks
    b. messages
    c. comments
7. Copy of Latest Program (Actual Coding)
8. Sample Run
    a. input
    b. output

Fun and Learning

I'm sure that every reader has played some kind of electronic game and knows that some of them get quite involved. Most serious computer buffs spend a few extra dollars to buy a game package for their computer. These enable you to play a simple game of tic-tac-toe or some very complex schemes like chess or "Star Trek." Many more will be on the market soon at very afford-able prices.

There are at least five magazines available in the field of "personal comput-ing" and you should subscribe to one or two. They have ads and new product listings for scads of fun things available at reasonable prices. Speaking of sub-scriptions, you should consider the following monthly publication:

Small Business Computers Magazine
SBC Publishing Co., Inc.
33 Watchung Plaza
Montclair, NJ 07042
(201) 746-4266

The magazine publishes a valuable annual survey of suppliers. The annual sub-scription is less than $20 and well worth the cost.

Another fun thing is buying presents for your computer. There is more hang-on stuff available than you can imagine and any retail computer store salesper-son can empty your checkbook faster than you can say megabyte. As a starter, you might consider an audio response unit. Some cost as little as $200 and will let you talk to your machine in a limited way. Don't get any delusions about having a machine like "Hal" from *2001: A Space Odyssey* or "Mother" from *Alien,* though.

The Paradox of Advancing Technology

Smith's Law #63 (actually Smith's Paradox) states, in summary, that we should never send a spaceship to the stars. Foolish? No, not really. Here's the logic behind that. Suppose that in the year 1985 we send a ship to Alpha Cen-tauri C, our nearest stellar neighbor—only 4.28 light-years away. Now, cosmo-logically, that's next door, considering that the diameter of the universe (if it's spherical) is five billion light years. Since light moves at 186,000 miles per sec-ond, Alpha Centauri C is 25,100,000,000,000 miles away. We will assume that the average velocity of our starship is 1 percent that of light. If the ship left earth in 1985, it would arrive in the star's orbital plane in the year 2413. Sup-pose that by the year 1995, we could launch a ship capable of 5 percent light speed. It would get there in 2080, beating the first ship by some 333 years! If we could attain 10 percent light speed by 2005, that ship would arrive in 2047, and so on. Continuing the logic of this obvious paradox to a fitting conclusion, we should never send a ship that far because a future one would catch and pass it and the equipment on board would be better also.

I've heard entrepreneurs use some of the same logic. "I'm going to wait a year or so until the price comes down." They get caught in Smith's Paradox. They never get there. The time is now! It's the only thing that you can both control and be sure of. Your competitor might have a computer already. If everything looks right, take the plunge. If Megalo Data Inc. comes out with a 29¢ computer next week, go buy that, too.

The End

For all practical purposes, this is the end of the book. I hope you have received value for your purchase and that you use what you have gained for your betterment and benefit. If you don't, then I've failed.

Appendix A is pure conjecture. My predictions could all be futuristic will-o'-the-wisps . . . but it could all happen just the way I say it will. You be the judge.

Appendix A   The Future of Small Business Computing

One of the most obvious changes in the shape of computer use in years to come will be the vast proliferation of computers in the home and in small business. What started as a hobby or a curiosity in the 1970's has become an operational reality. In the next ten years, the small computer will become an almost indispensable tool in every conceivable category of small business—from the gas station to the gastronomic enterprise. By 1990, almost any small operator that runs his or her business without some form of data or word processing will be severely hampered from a competitive standpoint. Not only will the cost of operating a non-computerized business rise rapidly, but the effective and essential use of time will have a significant impact on the successful operation of the venture. Time, it is said, is the one commodity that we all possess equally—168 hours per week, no more, no less. As the computer takes over more and more of the repetitive, time-consuming jobs in a small business, the owner or owners will be freer to devote more energy to planning, growth, and return on investment.

One area that we have not yet touched on is that of simulation. Computer simulation is a fascinating field. The computer creates hypothetical situations and then analyzes what occurs as a result of changing certain assumptions. For instance, it is now possible to assess the consequences of a business expansion on sales, expenses, capital investment, and profits. As they become more comfortable with their small computers, many entrepreneurs will be simulating future possible courses of action as they may affect the business. There are a few applications packages now that allow a small-business owner to make various changes in expense items and the rate of growth of sales to determine what these levels of income and outgo actually do to future earnings. In the next several years, true simulation programs will become available which will allow a small-business owner to do such things as analyze alternate strategies in relation to changes in competition.

Not only will there be several *million* new computers around by 1990, many of them will be communicating with one another. This capability means that business A can order an item from business B and pay for that order with very little human intervention. If people can communicate over telephone lines, so can computers; in fact, they have been doing so ever since the 1960's. Some of the ramifications of this communication capability include:

Electronic Funds Transfer (EFT). The nation's banks have been working toward this concept for years and, although the problems are staggering in their proportion, should arrive close to full EFT by 1995 or so. Many large corporations now allow employees to have their paychecks deposited directly to their bank accounts; several stores in the country allow customers to pay for goods by EFT. Essentially, if a customer buys, say, $50 worth of groceries at an EFT supermarket, that amount is deducted from his or her bank account and added to the store's account—instantaneously, at the checkout counter. Cash will not totally disappear until well into the third millennium, but we will be moving toward a more cashless society in the years to come. Credit cards will still have a function for people who wish to delay payment but their use may decline. By the way, by 1990 or so, a clerk accepting a credit card will no longer have to call a toll-free number for credit authorization—customers will only have to speak their name into a receiver and the voice analysis computer will do the rest. There will be literally no opportunity for phony credit cards or forgery, since voice prints are as unique and revealing as fingerprints.

Small-business owners who are unable to deal with EFT by 1990 may find themselves on the outside looking in.

Data Bases. It is a time-honored concept that the more information business owners have at their disposal, the better prepared they are to make the right decisions. There is already a system being readied for the home known generically as videotex which allows a subscriber to telephone a local number to request information. The desired information is then displayed on their television set. This system is like having access to a big city library's information right at home. Videotex does not use a home's computer at the present, but the transition would not be a difficult one. Not too far away is the ability of a small business computer to "capture" and use parts of huge data bases. Suppose, for example, a small-business owner wanted to send a mailing piece to every real estate broker in the state of Oregon. Once tied into the proper data base by telephone, the computer could select the codes for "Oregon" and "real estate broker" and back would come mailing labels on the computer's printer. Naturally, the business would be charged for the service, but nevertheless, it would be cheaper and faster than ordering labels from a mailing list company.

Credit. TRW Credit Data in Orange, California, now keeps records on some 70,000,000 Americans. Because of the present ability of large computers to store massive amounts of information, these files at TRW contain more positive than negative data. If yours is the kind of business that might be able to take advantage of rapidly available credit information on a potential customer (an auto dealer, for example), then this nearly instant credit reference may become very important to your business so that sales are not lost. Credit references on businesses, such as those now provided by firms like Dun & Bradstreet, are also becoming computerized.

Hardware

Circuitry. In the last ten years, nearly everyone has become aware of what has happened to the size and the cost of basic electronic circuitry. Standard four-function calculators have changed from 35-pound devices that cost between $1000 and $2000, to units that weigh a few ounces and cost less than $5. The next transition, we are told, is a cardboard, disposable calculator for less than $1.00. The same has been true for computers. Circuitry has shrunk to such a large degree that the major limiting factor on the rapidity of computation is the fact that electrical signals can travel no faster than the speed of light—186,000 miles per second. If two electronic circuits are separated by one inch (about four centimeters), it takes one-tenth of a billionth of a second for an electrical signal to move between the two elements. Many scientists regard that as too long for tomorrow's world. Thus, the circuits will have to be packed even more densely than they are today, but that creates a secondary problem—one of how to dissipate the heat that would be produced. The problem will be solved, but we need newer materials.

Memory. Since the 1950's, computer memory has gotten cheaper and smaller—just like the circuitry. This trend will continue, but the changes from now until 1990 will not be as dramatic as they have been in the past. In terms of cost, memory capacity has been a limiting factor but this will no longer be true. After the year 2000 it may become possible to construct a small computer that has the same capacity as the human brain: about 10,000,000,000,000 bits.

Input/Output. The small, hard disk for small computers has been one of the latest commercial breakthroughs. These devices should become somewhat cheaper as time goes on, but don't expect drastic changes since a large part of the mechanism is mechanical. The recording medium may become more dense, allowing for a greater packing density, however. Printers may not get a lot cheaper or faster in the next few years, but they are getting "smarter." Many line printers today have small microprocessors built into them that help to set up and structure the print job to maximize output. Audio input and response units should see more widespread use over the next several years.

Software

The applications that can be dreamed up in a small business are limited only by the human mind. Already there are more commercially available applications packages than many business owners could ever use and more are coming.

One interesting twist to programming is software routines that do a great deal of self-programming. A "master" program is loaded into the computer. By giving this program general descriptors and constraints regarding what it is that the programmer would like to do, it is possible to create most of a new program by drawing on and adapting "modules" or pieces of prewritten software. The era of mass-produced, yet customized, software is already here. Software in the 1980's and 1990's will become more universal, more integrated, and much easier to run and understand. By the mid-1980's there may be software available for small business that has "learning" capability, much like programs that have been written in years past that allow computers to "learn" to play chess by remembering all past defeats and what led up to them. Also, programming languages will begin to look more like English.

By the way, in the far future—2050 or so—there will be little in the way of stored information the way that there is today. It is already senseless for math students to carry tables of the functions of angles or logarithms. Inexpensive calculators can create them. It may be possible for the software systems of the future to re-create an entire business.

The Ultimate Question

At some point, anyone who becomes familiar with the basics of computers always asks if or when the computer will have the capability of thought. Certainly computers can be programmed right now in such a way as to make most people believe that these machines are already capable of understanding and thought generation, but this is only a primitive simulation of the real thing. If the ultimate question—can computers think— were asked today the answer would be a definite No. Will they be able to think in, say, the next twenty years? Maybe. In the next fifty? Yes.

We are reaching the stage, if indeed we aren't already there, where man and the computer can be said to be symbiotic—each class depends upon the other for the continuity of its existence. Certainly if all the computers in the world disappeared tomorrow along with the knowledge to re-create them, man would not cease to exist on this planet, but his lifestyle would certainly change drastically. Soon it might be possible to develop a man-machine interface that would couple the ability of humans to generate thought with the computer's phenomenal speed of processing and vast, infallible memory.

What will most likely occur is that scientists will develop a three-dimensional memory cell with living tissue. These cells will have the ability to reproduce themselves and to transfer knowledge to their "offspring." The complex DNA molecule already fits this description, but we have a way to go before we wire a bunch of them together into some kind of a biological crystal computer resembling a model of the human brain.

If we do all this, and finally replicate the brain with some kind of synthetic approach, we may find ourselves faced with a strange and interesting paradox. If the ultimate evolution of today's computer is a human-like brain and we are successful in creating it, we might have to invent the computer again and the cycle will just continue. What a mess!

Closing Comments

I hope that this book has helped you to gain some basic knowledge about small business computing. What you do next is up to you. I am interested in any comments that you have about this book, or about computers in small business in general. Write to me in care of The Stephen Greene Press, Brattleboro, Vermont 05301.

Appendix B A Notepad for Computer Evaluation

This notepad is for the use of prospective computer systems buyers in evaluating systems at computer manufacturers' plants, retail outlets, and other sites.

Page 1

Date completed:_____

Computer Manufacturer:

Company:_____

Address:_____

City:_____   State:_____   ZIP:_____

Phone:_____

Contact at manufacturer's location:

Name:_____

Phone:_____

Local sales representative:

Company:_____

Address:_____

City:_____   State:_____   ZIP:_____

Phone:_____

Contact:_____

Page 2

Computer model:_____

Main memory size:_____   Kbytes____

Add time:_____ nanoseconds__

Equipment that comes with the basic computer:

____CRT/Keyboard   Screen size:_____ chars. by ____ chars.____

____Character printer   Speed:_____ chars./sec.

____Line printer   Speed:_____ lines/min.

____Floppy disk(s)   No. of disks:_____

                        Capacity of one disk:_____ Kbytes____

____Hard disk(s)   No. of disks:_____

                        Capacity of one disk:_____ Mbytes__

____Tape   Capacity:_____ Mbytes____

Cost of basic system: $_____

Optional equipment:

Item	Cost	Manufacturer
____Card reader	$_____	_____
____Paper tape reader/punch	$_____	_____
____Remote terminal(s)	$_____	_____
____Audio unit	$_____	_____
____OCR	$_____	_____

Page 3

_____ $ _____   _____

_____ $ _____   _____

_____ $ _____   _____

Total cost of basics and options: $ _____

Languages that can be used:

    ____BASIC/CBASIC   ____FORTRAN

    ____COBOL   ____PASCAL

    ____PL/1   ____RPG

    ____   ____

Applications packages:

Type	Supplier	Cost
___General ledger	_____	$ _____
___Inventory control	_____	$ _____
___A/P	_____	$ _____
___A/R	_____	$ _____
___Payroll	_____	$ _____
___	_____	$ _____
___	_____	$ _____
___	_____	$ _____

Does manufacturer/sales representative provide training?   ___Yes ___No

        Cost: $ _____

Maintenance: $ _____   per month

Maintained by: _____

Other notes:

Appendix C Bibliography

BLUESTONE, M. D. and MAUTNER, R., *How to Program Computers in COBOL* (New York: Macmillan, 1974).

CARVER, D. K., *Introduction to Business Data Processing* (New York: John Wiley & Sons, 1979).

COAN, JAMES S., *Basic BASIC* (Rochelle Park NJ: Hayden Book Co., 1978).

DOCK, V. THOMAS, *FORTRAN IV Programming* (Reston VA: Reston Publishing, 1976).

FREIBERGER, S. and CHEW. P., *A Consumer's Guide to Personal Computing and Microcomputers* (Rochelle Park NJ: Hayden Book Co., 1978).

LEWIS, TED, *How to Profit From Your Personal Computer* (Rochelle Park NJ: Hayden Book Co., 1978).

KLOEK, CHRISTOPHER D., *Winning the Computer Game* (Santa Barbara CA: DDC Publications, 1978).

SILVER, GERALD A., *Small Computer Systems for Business* (New York: McGraw-Hill, 1978).

WARREN, C. and MILLER, M., *From the Counter to the Bottom Line* (Portland OR: Dilithium Press, 1979).

133

Appendix **D** Glossary

The following list of terms includes some of the jargon unique to computers, and specifically to smaller computers. The list is included both for reference purposes and for general reading and awareness on your part. It does not include every term that you will hear, but it will help to reinforce your knowledge. (Words in **boldface** type are themselves included in the glossary.)

Access Time The time, usually expressed in **micro**seconds or **nano**seconds, to get data from a computer storage device, like a **disk**, and bring it into the **CPU**.

Accumulator A **register** in the computer used to hold the results of arithmetic calculations, like the total of two numbers, for further computations.

Address The numerical designation that represents a physical **location** within a computer.

Add time Usually, the time, expressed in **micro**seconds or **nano**seconds, to add two one-digit numbers.

Alphanumeric Means, simply, made up of letters and numbers. The designation *A407BC27* is an alphanumeric **word**.

And A logical function or operation, performed by a computer, which follows the rule: "If both of the **inputs** are 1, then the **output** will be a 1; if either of the inputs or both is 0, then the output is a 0."

ANSI American National Standards Institute, which defines certain standard practices including **EDP** standards.

135

Applications Software Computer **programs** written to perform actual tasks, such as accounts payable or payroll in a business application.

Arithmetic/Logic Unit The physical part of the computer that performs mathematical functions (add, subtract) and makes **logical decisions** (is x larger than y?).

ASCII The American Standard Code for Information Interchange, a standardized, 128-item **alphanumeric** and symbolic set of **characters** used by computers.

Assembler A **program** which converts data and instructions in an **assembly language** to **machine** or **binary language**, which a computer actually processes.

Assembly Language A programming language that is positioned between a **high-level language** like **BASIC**, and **binary** computer code. Most assembly languages use a combination of commands (like ADD) and numerically-coded instructions.

Audio Unit The general term used to describe a computer accessory, or **peripheral,** which accepts or transmits the human voice sounds.

BASIC Beginners All-Purpose Symbolic Instruction Code—a popular, easy-to-learn, high-level programming language used in most small computers.

Batch Processing The term used to describe computer processing which works on one job at a time; opposed to **multiprocessing,** in which several jobs are performed by a computer simultaneously.

Baud Transfer rate of information in **bits** per second. A transmission device specified as 2400-baud moves data at 2400 bits per second.

Binary A numbering system which has the base 2; compare the commonplace decimal system, base 10.

Bit Binary Digit—a zero or a 1—the fundamental unit of computer-coded words, analogous to a letter, though bits do not contain real letters, only zeros and ones.

Bootstrap A **program** or a piece of computer **hardware** that gets other processing started.

Bug An unwanted function in **hardware** or **software** that has to be fixed to assure proper processing.

Bus An electrical conductor within the computer that is used to transmit information or power.

Byte Eight **bits** (usually), often also called a **word** in binary computer code.

Cassette A general term usually used to describe a self-contained magnetic tape that can be inserted easily into the drive unit of a computer.

CBASIC Commercial **BASIC**. CBASIC is a compiled language that has more flexibility than BASIC.

Character Any letter, number, symbol or punctuation mark that can be transmitted as **output** by a computer.

COBOL Common Business-Oriented Language, a high-level programming language that is used primarily with larger computers.

Compiler A computer **program** which translates an entire program written in a high-level "compiled" language, like **COBOL**, to binary-coded **machine language**, all in one pass. (See **Interpreter**.)

Control Unit The part of the **CPU** that regulates the operation of all the other physical elements within the computer.

Controller A piece of **hardware** that usually monitors the use of **input** and **output** equipment.

CPU Central Processing Unit. Collective term for the **Main Memory, Arithmetic/Logic,** and **Control** units of a computer; that is, the computer system *excluding* **input** and **output** devices, and **peripherals.**

CRT Cathode Ray Tube, also called the "tube," or the "screen," for video display of **output**.

Custom Software Computer **programs** prepared for a specific purpose. Opposed to **package software**, in which programs are written in advance.

Data Base A term used variously to describe the total collection of information available to a **program** or collection of programs.

Debug To fix errors in a **program**.

Dedicated If a computer or a piece of **hardware** is assigned exclusively to one task, it is said to be a dedicated system. In telecommunications, a dedicated line carries only one signal (compare a "non-dedicated" line, like a telephone circuit).

Diagnostics Computer **programs** that aid a programmer in finding mistakes.

Disk An **input/output** device that consists of a flat platter covered with a magnetic recording medium. There are fixed or **hard disks** and **flexible** or **floppy disks** also called diskettes. Flexible disks are more apt to be used with small computers than hard disks; but hard disks can hold more data than floppies can.

Dump A printed record of a section or all of a computer's internal memory.

EBCDIC Extended Binary-Coded Decimal Information Code, one of the most common sets of **character** codes used in computing.

EAM Electric Accounting Machines. The general classification for nearly obsolete card handling equipment, also known as "unit record" or tabulating equipment.

EDP Electronic Data Processing. Generic term for computers and their uses, also abbreviated to DP.

Error Message A one-sentence statement by the computer to the operator that something has been done incorrectly, i.e., "Does not compute."

Error Routine This is **software** which helps to find mistakes.

File A collection of **records** grouped under a common heading. For example, when all the inventory items and their respective counts are assembled, they become the inventory file.

Firmware A term used instead of either **software** or **hardware** that denotes **programs** permanently placed within a computer's circuitry; notably read-only memory (**ROM**) circuitry.

Flexible Disk See **Disk**.

Floppy Disk See **Disk**.

Flow Chart A diagram of separate blocks that graphically shows how a computer **program** works.

FORTRAN FORmula TRANslation, a high-level scientific programming language, not widely used with small computers.

Half Adder The basic computational device, or circuit, within a computer, which carries out the operation of addition on binary-coded numbers.

Hard Copy Computer **output** in printed form.

Hard Disk See **Disk.**

Hardware The physical parts of a computer; compare **Firmware**; **Software.**

High-Level Language Languages such as **BASIC, COBOL, FORTRAN** other than **assembly** or **machine languages.**

I/O Input/Output—usually refers to either an I/O device, like a **disk,** or to data itself.

IC Integrated Circuit, an entire complex electronic circuit on a small chip or piece of semiconducting material like germanium or silicon.

Input Any information coming into a computer.

Interpreter A computer **program** that converts into **machine language,** as it receives it, each instruction of another program, written in a high-level "interpreted" language like **BASIC.** The interpreter translates one instruction at a time; contrast the working of the **compiler** program, where the computer reads the program in the compiled language in its entirety before it begins to convert it into machine language. (See **Compiler**)

Interface Usually a piece of equipment that makes two computer units (like a **CPU** and a **printer**) able to work in tandem.

Keyboard Normally a set of **alphanumeric** and symbolic **characters** that are produced by striking keys. The keyboard itself is similar to that of a typewriter.

Key Pad A **keyboard** which is totally numeric (0–9) and resembles a calculator.

K Abbreviation for *Kilo-,* prefix meaning *thousand.* Hence a computer **main memory** specified as *64K* has a capacity of 64,000 **bytes.**

Load To enter data or instructions into a computer.

Location The physical place in a computer's memory, reached by an **address,** where an item of information is stored.

Logic The term used to designate that part of a computer's circuitry that makes **logical decisions** (e.g., x is greater than, lesser than, or equal to, y).

Logical Decision The capability of a computer to decide if one quantity is greater than, equal to or less than another quantity and then to use the outcome of that decision as a cue to proceed in a given way with a **program.**

Machine Language A language which consists of binary notation (0's and 1's) which can be understood directly by a computer, as opposed to **assembly** or a **high-level language.**

Mainframe Most popularly, a synonym for the **CPU.**

Main Memory The internal memory of the computer contained in its circuitry, as opposed to **peripheral** memory (tapes, **disks**).

Mega- Prefix for *million.* Hence 1 *megabyte* equals a million **bytes.**

Menu A list of **programs** or applications that are available by making a selection. For example, a small home computer might display the following menu: "Do you want to: 1. Balance checkbook? 2. See appointments for May? 3. See a recipe? Type number desired."

Merge A computerized process whereby two or more **files** are brought together by a common attribute, as Zip codes in ascending numerical order are used to merge a customer file with, e.g., a file of Aged Accounts Receivable.

MICR Magnetic Ink Character Recognition, a method of reading data using special **alphanumeric characters**. Usually used by banks to read checks.

Micro- Prefix for *millionth*. Hence a *microsecond* is a millionth of a second.

Microcomputer Generally, a small computer—smaller than a **minicomputer**.

Milli- Prefix for *thousandth*.

Minicomputer A small computer, intermediate in size between a **microcomputer** and a large computer.

Modem Modulator/Demodulator, a device that allows a computer to send and receive information, usually over telephone lines.

Multiprocessing The ability of a computer to work on more than one job at a time; opposed to **batch processing.**

Nano- Prefix for *billionth*. Some computers now process in *nanoseconds*.

Nibble Half a **byte** or four **bits**. Also spelled *nybble*.

Object Program A **program** in machine-readable form. A **compiler** translates a **source program** into an object program.

OCR Optical Character Recognition. The ability of a computer **peripheral** to read printed **characters.**

On Line A device like a TV or **CRT** that is directly connected to a computer and has access to the computer is said to be on line.

Or A logical function performed by a specific piece of computer circuitry that operates on the principle that if either **input** or both inputs are 1, then the **output** is a 1, otherwise the output is a 0. See **And.**

OS Operating System, the master piece of computer **software** which helps in controlling the operation of the computer.

Output Any processed information coming out of a computer, via any medium: print, **CRT,** etc.

Package Software See **Custom Software.**

Peripheral A device that is not an integral part of a computer, but works in conjunction with it, like a **printer** or **CRT.**

Printer A computer **output** device that produces written copy.

Print Out Printed information (**hard copy**) produced by a computer's **printer.**

Program A written set of instructions in a code that can be understood by a computer, and which carries out some task.

RAM Random-Access Memory. A system for retrieving data from a computer's memory, usually employing a **disk** as opposed to a tape, which provides *sequential* access memory.

Read Said of a computer, to *read* is to pick up data from tape, **disk**, card, etc., and store and/or process it.

Real Time An event, like a sale, is recorded, and the **record** is processed by a computer, in *real* time when the processing follows the event itself with little or no delay. The account of the sale, then, is available immediately after the sale, rather than, say, the next month.

Record A collection of **bytes** that together comprise an item that can be identified, like the name of each item in inventory and the count of items on hand. (See **File**.)

Register A temporary **location**, within a computer, which holds data.

ROM Read-Only Memory, internal computer memory which can be used to **read** from but not to enter data. ROM is fixed instructions and cannot be altered.

Service Bureau A company which provides programming services, but does not sell **hardware**.

Software A generic term referring to all kinds of computer **programs**. See also **Firmware** and **Hardware.**

Soft Copy Information displayed on a **CRT**. See **Hard Copy.**

Source Program A **program** written in a language that is not directly readable by a computer; it must be converted to an **object program** for use by a computer.

Sort To manipulate data in such a way that it has order, as in arranging a **file** of all customers in alphabetical order.

Throughput A term generally used to refer to the rate at which a computer processes information.

Time Sharing The use of a computer by two or more parties or customers.

Turnkey A computer system that when delivered or installed is ready to run without additional programming.

Utility Normally, a **program** which is a part of the **OS** and performs a specific task. A **sort** routine is a utility.

Video Unit A **CRT** or a TV set being used as a CRT.

Word In computer jargon, usually a **byte,** but the term can be used to designate any group of **characters** treated as a single unit.

WP Word Processing. A computer function in which printed words are generated and/ or manipulated. For example, a WP **program** might be instructed to make corrections in a printed text it had generated, and then to run the corrected text.

Write To permanently place data somewhere, as on a **disk** or tape.

Index